The Real Journey
of the
Empowered
Momboss

The Real Journey of the Empowered Momboss: Copyright @ 2018 Heather Andrews

www.heatherandrews.press

www.followitthru.com

Compiled by Heather Andrews:

www.heatherandrews.press

www.followitthru.com

Book and cover design by Lorraine Shulba: www.bluebugstudios.com

Editing by Amanda Horan: www.amandahoranediting.com

Zoey Duncan https://zoeyduncan.wordpress.com/

Ghostwriting by Suzanne LaVoie: www.suzannelavoiewrites.com

Manuscript formatting and compilation by Bojan Kratofil:
https://www.facebook.com/bojan.kratofil

ISBN: 978-1-5136-2929-2

Gratitude

I remember the day I published my first compilation called *Obstacles Equal Opportunities* in June 2017. That book was a turning point in my business and in my life; it set the platform that was to come.

I was grateful for the co-authors that shared their stories in the book and the shifts that happened to each of us afterward. Some of us went into a business venture together and met for the first time in January 2018. Others moved forward in their businesses because they believed in their capabilities. If you can become an international bestselling author on release day, imagine what else is possible!

As I launched that book in June 2017, I was going through so many of my own trials and tribulations as a mom and entrepreneur, I knew there had to be others in this world that felt like me. Even though my kids are older, my role as a mom is always needed; to listen, to support, help reduce stress, meal prep, workout with my kids and just hang out.

The one thing I am always grateful for their support and love they show in me as I grow my business.

When I began to ask other entrepreneurial moms about their journey, I noticed all the lessons we had all learned, the overwhelm on some days and the magic (or lack of) as we tried to juggle it all.

I found that the world is shifting and more women are making the change to reduce work hours and work from home or to work from home completely. As I began to look at information in the marketplace, I found there were a few books, but nothing like I wanted. So I decided to create one, the go-to guide for how eighteen women used the digital age to create their businesses, connect with other people, gain clients, create community and manage to keep their families thriving.

Through my community, I was referred eighteen beautiful, talented and influential women that have shared their stories with you in our book. I am so grateful for each of them as they share a piece of themselves with you through their lessons learned, adversities and celebrations of being a momboss.

I am grateful for my team that has brought this book to life as teamwork makes the dream work.

Thank you to each of our readers that supported and shared our book with family and friends, we all work together to create a better tomorrow.

Hugs,

Heather

Table of Contents

Foreword

As the world constantly changes around us, and technology takes over and evolves, the one thing that remains constant and that requires you to be always there in person is being a mom.

The internet has changed the course of our lives. How we do business and speak to each other now is far from how we spoke to each other in 1985. Back in those days if you wanted to speak to somebody halfway across the world, you only had two choices.

1. Run up a rather EXPENSIVE landline bill because mobile phones didn't exist.

   or

2. Board a plane and travel halfway around the world.

There was no turning on your PC/Mac and signing into your Skype account to chat to your client face to face on a computer screen, even though they may live 6,000 miles away. That simply didn't exist back then, and this made it even harder for moms to run a business from home.

Fast forward thirty years and it's a completely different world. While teenagers are totally obsessed with sharing bathroom selfies, moms are running businesses from home and getting paid extremely well for doing so.

However, she still needs to master the art of providing solutions to problems, know how to appeal to a target market, and learn exactly what emotion to trigger so that her customers click on that buy button, all while keeping her home in good order and being the mom her kids deserve.

We have gotten to a stage in advanced technology where we no longer need to go out the front door to earn money, buy clothes, or even eat. Every need can be catered for, which allows more stay-at-home moms to work from home than ever before.

I started my own online business seven years ago and never looked back, but the one thing I have learned across those seven years is how important balance is to a working mom and how we must keep ourselves in check to maintain that balance. It's so easy to get completely distracted from one area of your life and focus too much on the other, which then leaves the family side and home neglected. I know this from experience. At one stage, I let my business take over my life. The scales tipped way over, and the reality of that sucked!

I became ill; my relationship with my husband and kids STANK! I had to face the reality of the workaholic I had become, which was far from easy! Was running a seven-figure publishing house worth losing my health and family relationships? No! It wasn't, and so I checked myself into therapy and coaching and started working on restoring my balance in my life and started mastering the art of making time my slave.

Along my therapy journey, I learned the only reason why I was high achieving so much was to fill the hole of abandonment from my childhood. I had to learn I was enough and accept that I am doing more than my fair share of placing my mark on the world in my books and my consulting. I don't need to go that extra mile and kill my relationships and myself in order to succeed.

It took a long time to come to this place of balance for me and to really find that place of staying grounded as a business owner, and more importantly, a mom who is there for her children.

After making many mistakes, learning, and growing I made it to that place. To see this book placed in the world today really provides work from home moms with hope that you can find the right balance, that you don't have to feel guilty, and finally that you can leave a legacy without it completely taking over your life and your family.

Here's to your success (and balance).

God bless you!

Kate Batten

18 x international bestselling author, publishing specialist and publisher of The Missing Piece book series.

www.katebatten.com

Introduction

I heard a great quote this weekend that made me cry. 'Be the type of mom that your kids will brag about!'

I never thought I would be a mom as I was career driven and I wanted my life to be about me.

Then that fateful day in the desert of Saudi Arabia when I met my husband to be, I was hooked like an anchor on the sea floor.

He followed me home to Canada and together we raised three amazing teens. My youngest child will tell you as he told me, "Mom, you are the best mom, but you are not the typical one."

This made my heart sing as it meant that I'm teaching my kids that it's ok to move away from the norm. They can dream a bigger dream for themselves, and one day, for their families.

That is my vision for this book, *The Real Journey of the Empowered Momboss*. It is the journey taken or dreamed about by many women. They want to create their own vision or business so they can be at home with their kids or grandkids. They want to teach and help other women move into that place of the empowered momboss.

This journey, when chosen tests you; it brings the lessons into your life that you need to learn. Mindset, self-worth, self-esteem, financial management, and self-belief. These are just a few obstacles that the universe put on my path and the paths of my fellow authors.

I wanted to create a book that brought women together to share their journey of entrepreneurship while juggling children, finances, partners, and work. All while having fun and using the power of the digital age to connect with people and build their businesses.

These stories from our wonderful co-authors, which are raw and shared from each of their hearts, will help other women learn to use the digital age to create a business they are proud of. It will help to guide you and provide the tools you'll need to move through the different phases of being a momboss while your family continues to thrive.

This will be the go to book for mombosses who want to elevate their business while raising their family without the guilt and overwhelm.

The stories are real and the tools are tried and tested.

Come with us on this journey and find the 'aha' moments that will help you live your desired life.

Hugs,

Heather

Heather Andrews

Lifestyle strategist, certified Follow It Thru health coach and international bestselling author, Heather Andrews initially created the inspiring Mom On The Go change mentorship program in a bold, immediate response to being 'restructured' out of her 'dream' management position in the beleaguered healthcare system. She was unaware of the extent of her resiliency or what this confidence-shattering experience would uncover.

Heather's veritable 'rediscovery' of her self-esteem, and her journey to the realization of a deeper, personal identity led her to ultimately embrace entrepreneurship wholeheartedly. With her own publishing company, and bestseller based on her signature story, *Obstacles Equal Opportunities*, as well as a foray into podcasting and internet radio, where she will host her own show, Follow It Thru to a Stellar Life. As a speaker, Heather inspires audiences by sharing her challenges and the survival strategies that continue to help her optimize adversity. Being a voice in self-discovery and revitalization, she is making a positive difference.

Find Heather online:

Websites: www.heatherandrews.press
www.followitthru.com
Facebook: www.facebook.com/followitthru

Chapter 1

My Self-Worth Reclaimed

By Heather Andrews

I stood on the stage in Miami, holding my arms in the air with one-hundred people in front of me applauding after giving a good speech. I was proud and ever so grateful for the opportunity. This is someone's dream, and I thought I was living mine. However, something did not feel right in my gut. I did not know exactly what it was, but my heart and head did not align. I had been in my business for one year, and I was so proud of what I had created, especially after what I had endured the year before.

People always told me I was a born speaker. Yes, I had the gift of the gab, and I facilitated meetings in my job. However, I discovered one thing that day; it was very different getting up in front of people to speak about your business and have people believe what you are teaching while finessing the skill of speaking at a professional level.

Little did I know what the next year would bring. What I did know were the lessons I had learned up to this point as an entrepreneur in business were life-altering. I was paving my new path.

You see, I thought my future was pretty much set before I was restructured out of my dream role. That was how my entrepreneurial experience began. I knew in my heart I was being given a new opportunity, but without my job title, I did not know who I was. That was when I began to reclaim my identity.

I had put who I was, my internal self-worth, my external confidence and faith into my job title. So where did that leave me if I was without it? Well, it left me feeling like a culprit had stolen my identity, the same as if they had stolen my social security number and emptied my bank accounts. I felt in my gut that my restructuring was looming. I came up with a plan B but I was not prepared for the emotional curveball that came with the restructuring.

I went home that fateful day and spoke to my husband and kids about my plan B:

1. I was going back to school for my health coaching certification because coaching and mentoring were my favorite part of being a leader.

2. I was going to create more than one revenue stream. The fact that someone had control over my income and that they could take it away in one minute scared me to death.

3. I was not working in a full-time job for one company ever again.

4. I knew at forty-five years old, I wanted my own business and to maintain my professional designation.

5. I knew it was my time to model a different way for my kids. Telling them that I had been laid off were some of the most

difficult words I have had to say. They are young adults, and we always had open communication, even when they were little and their dad was deployed.

Plan B went into effect. My husband, John, knows me well enough to just nod and say, "I love you dear."

My kids: eighteen, fifteen, and thirteen were a bit apprehensive, but they said, "We believe in you, Mom."

I used my severance package money to go back to school for my health coaching certification, which took about one year. I landed a couple of per diem contracts that kept me working on a flexible schedule. My Plan B was working out for me. About six months into school, I launched my website and hired a business coach. I even had a few clients by this time; granted they were not paying me a lot, as I did not think I was good enough to charge more. In my mind, I was rocking it both professionally and entrepreneurially. I was completing the tasks my coach gave me. I did online research to figure out what my target market was, my niche, and what the needs were in respect to the coaching program I was creating. I discovered that busy entrepreneurial moms needed guidance and support for stress management, boundary setting, communication skills, time management, and self-care. Hence, the Mom on the Go program was launched.

My business coach had her event in Miami, and she invited me to speak. I was honored and excited, yet as I walked off the stage, my gut feeling was off. In reflection, I know why, but back then, I was unaware that every lesson I created in my program, the universe was going to teach me over the course of the next year.

My business coach was launching her own year-long long mastermind. My gut screamed, *You must do this,* as once again, I wanted my business to thrive so badly and I did not feel like I could do it on my own. I made the investment. To me it was no different from investing in going back to school.

Upon arriving home, I knew I needed to figure out why I did not feel aligned with my business. I loved what I did, and coaching was my jam, so what was wrong?

Over the next month, I was like a squirrel and could not focus. I started everything but never finished anything. I hired a company to help to finish out my web design and sales funnels, and I kept changing my mind about things. People kept saying I needed to focus one thing at a time, but I have *never* been a one-thing kind of girl. In my management role, I always handled numerous amounts of projects, and I had the skill set to handle it. What was wrong with me now? I kept asking myself, but the answers never came, or maybe I refused to listen to them, or I was scared to look within myself to find the answer (EUREKA – winning answer).

One of my turning points occurred when I finally had a coaching call with the mindset expert as part of the mastermind I was in. She asked me point blank, "Where is your power?" I said, "What?" Then it hit me like a freight train going full speed. The day of my restructuring, I left my power at the door. I needed to bring my corporate self, my creative clock and internal drive to my business. I also realized I let someone outside of me take away my self-worth. Things started to change the next day, I felt like I had lost 20 lbs.

Then, out of the blue, my friend asked me to be a part of a women in business compilation book to be launched on Amazon. I had a very successful business in my thirties, and my husband was deployed to Afghanistan. I became a solo parent to three kids; I made it work. I dived in and wrote like crazy. I asked my kids if it was ok to be in this book because part of my story would be about them. They were so excited for me and it was such a healing outlet. Much to my surprise, I found that I could write. The benefits of taking a leap of faith was met wonderful women who have now become friends, joint venture partners, and business partners. As a result of that book becoming an international bestseller, I realized the power of connection and belief in one's self. The lessons of my twenties and thirties were showing up in my forties to teach me courage, healing, and growth.

I expanded my network triple fold, restructured my coaching program, was interviewed on nine radio shows, and stepped out of my comfort zone to speak at local events. Kate Gardner, the publisher who wrote the foreword in this book, launched her publishing mentorship program. I said to myself, I want to do this. We talked, and BOOM, I was going to learn how to be a publisher and compile my own book.

All the while, I am still raising my three children, working my contracts, relaunching my coaching program and learning in this mastermind program. When I talk about raising my children, they are teenagers, self-sufficient, but they still need their mom. Even though I am not always around due to travel or pouring hours into my business, my mom and husband have been an incredible support. My kids know I love them, have their back and am available by text or phone when I am away.

On April 2017, twenty-two beautiful, soulful people joined me in my compilation, and we created our book *Obstacles Equal Opportunities*, which became a bestseller on its release day. My favorite part of that day was my kids sharing my posts on social media. The comment went like this, 'My mom is a true inspiration and she models the way for us'.

Reclaiming my life was the best gift I could give them. That day, Follow it Thru publishing was born. Was I ready to do this? No. Did I know what I was doing? Sometimes, but I had support. Did it feel great, and with ease and grace? Yes! I found my home. I found the business that I was meant to be doing.

After the book launched, I focused on my coaching program and finished out the mastermind program I was in because I had lost some traction. I started to put myself down for not always being fully present. However, I then realized that I made a very conscious choice to learn publishing and take a step back from coaching. I know why it happened; it is what I am meant to be doing. Yet, there was still something screaming at me from deep inside that there was more to learn. Deep down, I always felt like I needed to know more before I could become an expert. It was as if there was a little birdie on my shoulder saying, "You still don't know enough." I knew it all along, and I kept spending money to learn and have others help me because that was what I needed.

During the summer and fall, I had enrolled in three very different styles of transformation courses. I invested over one-hundred hours of learning about my soul, my self-worth, my heart, my head, and my belief in self. I began trusting in myself again. I learned that I could not commit to anything because I did not value myself enough. I gave to everyone else before I took time to ask for what I needed. I cried for days. I let go of crap from my dad's death, my stepfather's death, my first marriage, and harbored resentment of my husband's deployment. All of it! GAME CHANGER!

From what I have been through and learned about myself, I have always taught my children the best with what I knew, especially when their father deployed to Afghanistan. The day I knew I was deeply changed was the day one of my kids came to me in tears after a rough day to state that they did not think they would ever be good enough to do anything. I asked questions and I shared openly about my journey, which is something I would have never done before. I asked if he would create a list of the top twenty-five things he believed about himself. I told him what I saw, and there was hope in his eyes. My child read his list of twenty-five traits with the power of 'I AM'. I AM STRONG, I AM HONEST...the list went on.

Each day my kid read his list as part of increasing belief and confidence. The shift started, knowing I had his back, love him, and that he could come to me. What made it better was I had a tool from my own coaching practice and self-discovery that worked. That is what makes it real, authentic, and heart driven.

Finally, I aligned myself with a team of business soulmates, and we coach each other through our times of discovery and growth. It has been outstanding. I changed companies to hire another team that can help and implement my vision. My husband is now on board too. He has been silently supportive, but trust me, we have had our share of discussions over the money I invested.

With their support, my self-discovery, and getting out my own way, I began to believe in myself again.

In seven months, I have launched my publishing company and released multiple books from compilations and solo-authors. I have added services to my publishing company with an amazing team, revamped my coaching program with successful client's outcomes (including my own), started a radio show, and bought a podcast network so I can introduce audiobooks as part of my publishing company.

My vision is to help people bring their stories to life in a novel way, through print and voice, to reach the masses who need to know they are not alone.

I got my health and wealth on track because I hired a trainer and started using essentials oils and a weight management line, which

I have created income streams from. I made sure to keep my promise to myself in regards to having multiple income streams.

I am a publisher, author, coach, business owner, speaker, teacher, and lifestyle strategist.

Most importantly, I am worthy and deserving.

I have learned a ton along the way, but I still encountered obstacles in my path.

1. I hit my emotional bottom of anger and lack of self-worth as I was triggered by previous lifetime experiences, but I made my comeback.

2. I did my business start-up all wrong with a ton of debt, but today I am finally on a business loan repayment plan.

3. I invested money in people because I wanted them to believe in me. I thought I couldn't do it on my own. Now I believe in my capabilities wholeheartedly and without question.

4. After rebranding four times with obstacle after obstacle in my way, I have learned lessons that made me drop to my knees to surrender and trust in my journey as an entrepreneurial momboss with more opportunities that I can handle.

5. I lacked clarity of my purpose and trust within myself. People knew I did not believe in myself enough to charge for services rendered. I appeared disorganized and scattered because I wanted to do everything to show the world that I was still worth something. This meant that I never finished what I started.

That is the overview of what the last three years have been like, and honestly, I would do it all over again without question because I figured out who I was, my core values, and what I stand for. I modeled the way for my children and their children for generations to come. That may sound cliché, but that is ok. I have never been as emotionally, mentally and physically strong. I am finally living my stellar life.

I am thankful for this profession called entrepreneurship and believe more people should be one, or attempt to be one. This will teach you more than the courses you take in school. I have learned perseverance and resilience. I am a better human, mom, wife and coach, and I've fallen in love with life again because of it.

I never thought there were differences between the corporate world and owning your own business. Man, was I surprised. I feel like I should have walked across the stage for my degree by now. However, I know differently. The good lord is not done with me, I have more to learn and overcome if I truly want to reach my vision.

All I know is there was a plan to get me to this point for the last forty-five years. I have learned skills, fallen in love, had kids, hit rock bottom, changed jobs, experienced loss, completed certifications, owned my first business, and finally, started my publishing/coaching company. There is work for me to do and people to serve. My obstacles and opportunities led me here. The foundation is set, and my business is exploding. My kids are sharing my journey and even they say they look forward to running their mom's company one day.

I start each day with gratitude. I am forever grateful for what has happened, is happening and is going to happen.

Tell your story, inspire others, create new ones and change lives. That is being an empowered momboss.

Come with us, it is better over here.

Your choice☺

Lessons Learned and Mindset Tips

Lessons learned:

1. Create space to build something new in your life. Declutter your mind, house, and calendar.

2. Trust your gut.

3. Your self-worth of accepting, deserving and knowing that you can accomplish your goals is the essence and foundation of your life.

Mindset tips:

1. Be grateful.

2. Be kind in your self-talk.

3. Be intentional. Envision how each step feels and celebrate it.

Aha Moments and Self Reflections

Note your Thoughts

_____

_____

_____

_____

_____

_____

_____

_____

_____

_____

_____

_____

_____

_____

_____

_____

_____

_____

_____

_____

Apryl Dawn

Apryl has been an entrepreneur all of her adult life, owning the first of her four businesses by the age of twenty-one. She is an avid yogi, yoga teacher, legacy Lululemon ambassador, and now full-time jewelry designer for her own company Apryl Dawn Designs. She's self-grown her brand into an international name, selling in over forty-five stores from her home city of Calgary, Alberta, all the way to New York City and into Europe. She's had the pleasure of making custom pieces for a dragon from the hit entrepreneurial series Dragon's Den. Apryl has been featured in OK! magazine, Flare, and the talk show The Social. One of her proudest moments was being asked to participate in the 2015 Emmy's Style Lounge in L.A.

Currently a writer for a local magazine, designer, and single mama, Apryl is incredibly grateful for the life experiences that have crossed her path…knowing that it's within the fires of life where the best learning occurs.

Find Apryl online:

Facebook: https://www.facebook.com/IamAprylDawn/
Instagram: https://www.instagram.com/iamapryldawn/
Website: www.apryldawn.com

Chapter 2

Manifesting Through Fear

By Apryl Dawn

I want to tell you a story of a struggle, a struggle that led a woman to victory in her own life. It's a story about how the downs of life can be a tough, disciplined learning channel to an incredible life win, and how being a single mama doesn't inhibit growth, but gives you the momentum to fight.

I spent the first half of my life trying to cope with my environment, and this shaped a person that I didn't connect with in the least. I grew up with alcoholics as parents. There was no physical, emotional, or mental affection. No hugs and no I love you's. Survival was the name of the game and hiding the disease, and the embarrassment that came along with it became the rules of play. Lies and deceit covered up what was actually happening behind closed doors. The abuse was real, but the need to save face won. Moving constantly to run from the fires that were started, I lived in fear and instability.

My childhood was stolen before I ever had the chance to experience it. I could feel the walls of my life closing in on me, and at times, I couldn't see the light outside of what felt like my casket. I was born into a life that didn't leave much room for growth of any kind, and only paved a path for me to become a statistic. As we live in a constant state of chaos, and fighting to simply exist, the liberty of connecting to ourselves is consumed by the flames of our surroundings. How we choose to endure and learn from these years separates the happy and successful from the angry and stuck. I decided to choose to be happy.

I consciously made a choice when I was young to, as I phrased it as an eight-year-old, "do everything the complete opposite of my parents". My eight-year-old self wasn't foolish. I saw the unhappiness and misery that they created and surrounded themselves with. I could only imagine if I acted completely different, I would somehow find the path to contentment. I knew there would be an end to the madness somehow, as even at that age I knew that we lived in a state of impermanence. Everything ends eventually, and the tortuous cell I had been confined to would eventually break open. Despite knowing that needed to do things differently from my parents, I lost sixteen years in someone else's vicious reality. The day I moved out, I vowed that was the end of succumbing to someone else's forced reality for me.

Today, I thrive on constant change and chaotic situations. My upbringing was my education; however, this is no 'woe is me' type of story. This is a chapter of my life, that's for sure, but it isn't the story I choose to live in. I believe we are handed what we can handle, and if we handle it properly, we will use the dark places in our lives as tools for our futures.

I was a lost statistic, stuck in a prison of low self-worth, struggling to be anyone and anything so that I could feel a sense of belonging and love. The pain of it all was edged into my spirit, and really should have broken me, but miracles happen, and I slowly started to learn:

That we are creators and dreamers.

That WE own our own destinies.

That the bullshit that is placed on our path is there to be overcome and embraced.

To find happiness through the muck and mud of our lives.

To be the lotus flower.

These are all lessons, my friends, as harsh as they come, and we must be thankful for every bump, mountain, and gouge to our journeys. This is where the learning occurs. Every failure, rejection, and loss is an opportunity to receive valuable knowledge from the universe. Without the darkness in our lives, we would never really, truly appreciate and be grateful for the light. Without overcoming barriers and fears, and bulldozing walls placed in front of us, we would never know true accomplishment. It's all about how we handle it. I could have become a statistic. That would have been easier. I however, chose not to settle. My dreams kept me up at night; I knew I was destined for more. So I created more, and I followed my heart and soul to where I am today.

I fell into a yogic path, became a teacher, and have now been practicing for over fifteen years and teaching for seven. I thrive in that room, my therapy space. Yoga opened the door to the practice of manifestation. A practice I now speak and teach on, as well as being devout to within my own life. I am a firm believer that this practice caused me to soar when all that was expected was my crash. I want to take you on a journey through one of my proudest (so far) life-manifested creations.

I rebranded in the spring of 2015, as my 'hobby' of designing jewelry had quickly become more of a full-time gig. The first time I launched the new brand to the world was a small weekend market in July. I was set up beside a clairvoyant. She came over to tell me that this brand of mine, my jewelry collection was going to be big. Like BIG big, and in my manifestation mind, I thought, *well, obviously*! She continued to tell me that I would be making a mark from Los Angeles to New York and this was going to be something that happened quickly. September quick.

I left the market that weekend with a compelling feeling about what the clairvoyant had mentioned. So I began to meditate on it, and I started surrounding the month of September in my mind with the powerful feeling that I had deep inside. I surrounded this month with dynamic emotion, of feeling deep, beautiful shifts occurring. Change, transformation, Om Shreem Maha Lakshmiyei Swaha. I chanted the mantra of Lakshmi, the goddess of abundance, wealth and prosperity. I started to align my life with what it was I wanted to attract.

As a single parent, the struggle was real. I worked day and night for three years to build my business as a jewelry designer, all while teaching full-time yoga and being the best mama I could be. I would create jewelry after putting my son to bed; fulfill orders for the studios and stores that I was so grateful to have, and work every weekend I could at markets or teaching workshops. Something was working, but I was feeling unaligned, stressed and exhausted. My business kept growing and growing, but that just meant I slept less and less. I had zero time for anything other than my son and work, but even they didn't have the 'whole me' invested. A shift in my life had to happen. I needed to give up my yoga classes so I could make jewelry full-time. As a single parent to a then four-year-old, this was a terrifying option, but I am a firm believer in creating space for the new. If we are too full, we absolutely cannot accept the abundance that is waiting. So I threw caution to the wind, and I made space in my life for my passion project gone rogue, and opened my arms wide and yelled to the universe to fill them up again. Ohm Shreem Maha Lakshmiyei Swaha. Fill me with abundance goddess Lakshmi, you're all I have now.

Lakshmi answered in the form of an email I received early August. I had been invited to take part in a styling lounge for the Emmys. *Me*, I thought. *Little ol' handmade jewelry me?*

"Yes, you!" the universe answered. "Put on your big girl panties and let's storm this world," it screamed.

"OK," I said, "let's do this." No thinking, just doing. I planned my life around taking off for Los Angeles for the Emmys in under four weeks' time. This was life presenting itself in real form in a major way. Manifest, friends, manifest. It's not about waiting for something you ask for to drop suddenly from the sky, it's about living and breathing your dreams, and being in alignment with what you KNOW you deserve. I knew I was ready and deserving of what the psychic had told me, and it became my reality. I worked my ass off and flew to L.A. to set up for the Emmys weekend. I met celebrities, interviewed with major magazines such as Elle, In Touch, Forbes, US Weekly, OK! magazine and Flare. I pinched myself the entire time – it was surreal. It solidified that I had taken the advice of my former eight-year-old self, and made an authentic and palpable life out of the statistical fate that I was handed. However, it was what happened when I was home that sealed all my deals with the universe.

I came home from my high in L.A. to an immediate crash. This is bound to happen when you're walking on the clouds in la la land and come home to real mom and work life. I found my way out with a meditation and a commitment to a manifest that I was going to bring into existence: I wanted to be in print. There were dozens of online articles mentioning my company after the awards, but it didn't settle with me. I wanted more. I ALWAYS want more. I want to be intimate with the deepest version of any experience I can. I want the absolute most I can get out of every opportunity that is presented, and if you pay attention, there are opportunities EVERYWHERE. With this situation, I felt the most I could get out of it would be to see my name in print. To see my company in millions of copies of a magazine all over the world. Hardcopy. That's what little ol' me wanted, and I was going to get it. I meditated every day on it. I sat and felt what it would feel like to see myself in an international magazine, I trusted my intuition on this, and most importantly, I felt how immensely this was warranted. I have worked hard my entire life, and it was my time for something absolutely mind-blowing to happen. It was time for the chaos to turn into my favor. I deserved this. I knew I did. I knew this so deeply that I could literally taste that magazine in my mouth. Weird, right? Or is it? Remember that quote, 'Want something so bad you can taste it'? Well, this quote finally made sense at the age of thirty-four. "Gimme gimme," I chanted.

And I got it. I remember the moment with such clarity. I screamed in delight. I was alone, and I was screaming like a child. Crying. Goosebumps. Chills. Pure elation. *Me!*

Derek Hough from Dancing with the Stars was signing my banner, and this is the picture that graced the pages of OK! magazine. Right smack in between Gwen Stefani and Matt Damon, was my brand. My dreams, my mind, my jewelry company, in print. All of my hard work for the world to see. The only picture from the Emmys style lounge to make it into *any* magazine, and it was *my* brand. I'm still in awe. I'm just a girl from a small town who wasn't given an opportunity to succeed. A girl who had to fight hard to find her own way in a world that seemingly was against her. A war against adversity won and a smile to last for years and years was created. A huge building block in my mind to run head-on into everything I want to be and do, because I will. Why was my company chosen? Why me? Why that picture, and nobody else's? Why? Because I wanted it so bad, I put it out there. I designed my life around attracting this success into my life.

There is a fine line that separates the successful and the not so successful, and it's the fact that the successful believe in themselves. The successful take failure as a challenge and a learning point in life. They grieve it, and then they throw it in their fire and use that energy as fuel to move on, smarter than they were before the BS happened. The successful trust in themselves and their destiny, knowing that they themselves illuminate their own trail. Most importantly, the successful believe they are WORTH it. They are worth everything that they desire and dream. Despite how much work it will take, they know they will end up with their fantasies being their absolute truth.

Surround yourself with people who support your dream, no matter how crazy it seems. Eliminate negativity on all levels. Peel away each layer of your life and cleanse it. From friends to family, to social media, surround yourself with your worth. Get rid of the non-believers and the haters. You want to be respected for your hustle, your drive, and your ambition. Do not let that gloomy little voice in your head get the best of you, it's not actually you, it's a co-habitation of every shitty thing someone has thrown at you. Your heart and soul is you. Your dreams and your desires are you. Your spirit is you. Don't let the haters neutralize your glow. Your people are the ones who light you up, lift you up, and give you the power to become. We are constantly evolving in this wild world of ours. Check in with yourself, your life, and your surroundings. Are they vibing with what your heart and soul is aching for? Remember that your true capacity for success lies in your capacity to love yourself first.

This is just a chapter of my life. It isn't sad – it just started that way. I've embraced that I am here to live and love hard. All of our paths are made to be different, and nothing will ever be 'normal'. Remember that. Our paths are unique and different. There is no roadmap that will tell you the right way and lead you to your success. You will have to navigate this life from start to finish by trusting your guts, your intuition, and your heart. The ugly and the beautiful in life, nothing is set in stone except our relationship with our inner teacher and our authenticity of who we are. Be who you are unapologetically and without doubt. Come into union with life's path, love yourself to death, and remember what is right for you. Don't forget to live like you have nothing to lose, because what do you truly have to lose if you're not living?

"She was never crazy; she just didn't let her heart settle in a cage. She was born wild, and sometimes we need people like her. For it's the horrors in her heart which cause the flames in ours…and she was always willing to burn for everything she ever loved."

-R.M. Drake

Lessons Learned and Mindset Tips

Lessons learned:

1. Your 'story' and your past don't reflect your future.

2. Your gut is your intuition – trust it.

3. There are opportunities in every situation, be open to letting them in and 'seeing' them.

Mindset tips:

1. Always believe in your journey, the dark and the light, they are all part of the process. The darkness is where we learn the most.

2. Always say yes now, and figure it out later...that whole opportunity thing again!

3. Always face your fears, manifest through to the dreams on the other side. There are no dreams without fear in the beginning.

Aha Moments and Self Reflections

Note your Thoughts

Lisa Bovee

Lisa Bovee is badass mama, mimi, friend, and human. She lives, teaches, and writes in Austin, TX.

Lisa lost her twenty-two-year-old son, Conner, in a car accident the day after 'Thanksgiving', 2016. She now focuses on creating a legacy in her son's name (ConnerBoveeLove.org) by supporting, educating, and writing about grief and hosting global Grief Writing Journeys.

Lisa has been guided by grief to create a movement that changes the conversation about grief from private, ugly and uncomfortable to OPEN, NORMAL and SUPPORTIVE.

Join the movement!

Guided by Grief: Always Remember, is out now. The second book, *Guided by Grief: So Much Love,* launches in June 2018.

Lisa speaks on grief and loss and co-hosts a podcast called *Kicking Grief's Ass* with Conner's best friend, Steven.

Find Lisa online:

Website: http://guidedbygrief.com
Facebook: https://www.facebook.com/lisa.m.bovee
Podcast: Kicking Grief's Ass The
Podcast: https://soundcloud.com/user-960583321/sets/season-one

Chapter 3

Grief: A Life Repurposed

By Lisa Bovee

Remember Jean Naté? I *loved* the spray, the powder, the body wash – the everything. It felt *so fancy* to this little girl from Central Florida. One year, I received a Jean Naté gift-set for Christmas, and oh…the container it came in…ZOHMYGOD! Amazing (I have an unhealthy container obsession). The point: when we had garage sales, I would mind the money – I'm not sure why, because I'm terrible with money. But, I digress. I was minding the money and using my empty Jean Naté box as a 'cash register'. I put the money inside the molded plastic, and I would slide *that* part back into the outer cardboard box. Genius, right? I believe this seemingly silly moment was my entrepreneurial gateway, the realization that I had that 'entrepreneurial spirit'. I was twelve, the same time the dreaded "what do you want to be when you grow up?" question began.

Even though this undiscovered drive to use that spirit existed, I would inevitably answer, "I want to be a mom." *I want to be a mom.* Truly, that was my heart's greatest desire. While in school, I was a fantastic student: National Honor Society, the quintessential teacher's pet, and part of every club imaginable. Glee Club, yes kids, I said Glee Club. I was a proud member of Future Business Leaders of America, where I always won first place in mock interview contests, and I was a member of the Foreign Language Club. I spoke French and lived in France as an exchange student. I joined the Key Club, I sang in a Jazz ensemble, and I was a cheerleader. That was for *on-campus* activities. I also played softball outside of school. The pitcher's mound is where I spent most of my career. You get the picture – I was no slouch.

I was adopted at five days old, so I've often asked myself the nature or nurture question. I don't know my DNA recipe; therefore, 'nurture' seems rational. However, in order to relay the most accurate 'nurture' story, I must confess that I was raised in a stable yet chaotic environment. My coping mechanisms were staying busy, being the 'good girl', and not contributing further to my parents' stress. I either developed or was born with the mindset of an entrepreneur: dedicated, driven, and determined. Even so, I happily placed entrepreneurship (and college) on the back-burner while I raised my babies.

Food for thought: embrace lessons that come out of navigating difficult circumstances. Work hard. Go with your gut.

Fast forward: I had a husband, two daughters and one son by age twenty-four. Just like I was the quintessential teacher's pet, I was the quintessential stay-home-mom, school volunteer, and homeroom mom. I even coached my son's soccer team. Still fanning the flames of my entrepreneurial spirit, I sold Home Interiors.

My marriage wasn't perfect, but it was 'fine'. We had ups and downs, good and bad times, but eventually realized we were/are better apart – as friends and co-parents. Our separation and subsequent divorce were amicable, and I will always give my first husband kudos for taking care of us (financially). He respected the huge role I played in raising our children and made it possible for me to continue this important work, even after we separated. I am grateful. He knows, in case you're curious.

Food for thought: when divorce happens, I believe it's important to come away having learned lessons and striving to become a better partner, parent, and person.

Post-separation I was thirty-something, had three children, no college education, no earned-income and no career. Not uncommon, but what's a gal to do? While raising my kiddos, I dabbled. My best friend Marci's family needed help, so she and I helped run her family's thriving catering and event-planning company. We would trade several days a week: one would go to work, and the other would watch all five kids. I *loved* all of it. I adored taking care of all the kids and meeting with clients, finding the right space, and transforming it for their celebration. This experience offered valuable insight into running a business, interacting with clients, getting along with colleagues, working under pressure, sticking to a budget, and diffusing work-place spats.

Food for thought: the world is your classroom. Life is the course, but there is no textbook. Pay attention. Each moment presents valuable lessons.

Eventually, the catering company was sold, and a few years after that I connected with a fellow parent at my kids' elementary school. He and I hit it off and began spending lots of time together. Our relationship fluctuated between romance and friendship, and eventually, we added a business to our already convoluted situation. We did have similar goals around building a business, and we worked well together, but neither of us was sure which direction to go. He was big into motocross, and I began attending weekend races with him. I loved the revving of motors, the dirt, smoke, mud, and camaraderie. The atmosphere, competition, and testosterone! Pretty quickly, I was riding, and we built a business together in that testosterone-filled world.

We manufactured and sold glove-liners for endurance and long-distance motorcycle, motocross, ATV riders, and races. With my partner's guidance, I was heading up the professional manufacturing, and packaging the product (on my dining room table). One day, my phone rang; it was Rocky Mountain Distributors (an international distributor). They were interested in having our product! We struck a deal, and our liners were placed across America. In between helping the kiddos with homework, volunteering at school, making treats for the teachers and swapping kids for every-other-weekend visits to dad, I had happily entrenched myself as a business owner and an established professional woman, in 'a man's world'. I also landed endorsements from professional riders. How did I do that? One day, my biz partner suggested, "It would be cool if Ty Davis would endorse our product." I agreed.

I had previously sent Ty several pairs of gloves to try. I had seen him wearing them, so I knew he was using (and liking) them.

I called him. He answered. I asked. He said, "yes." Success!

Food for thought: having the courage to ask, in my opinion, is the greatest trait of anyone who wants to be successful in any arena – especially as an entrepreneur.

We were doing the entrepreneurial thing. I was proud and excited. Sadly, the pride and excitement were short-lived, and our endeavor was complicated by our fluctuating relationship cycles. I thought we were just business partners, but boy was I thrown for a loop when, after our success, my partner revealed to me that he was in love with me. I wish I could tell you the end was like a fairytale, and we lived happily ever after, but that's only in the movies! I was shocked and confused. After reflection, I dissolved the business and moved on.

Food for thought: when collaborating, have a *binding contract* and a clear exit strategy. My dissolution was swift and uncomplicated, but it could have gone sideways hard and fast. Hope for the best, prepare for the worse.

Extricated and fairly unscathed, I started a concierge company (Key Concierge), which was short-lived due to the recession. Then, I decided it was time for that college degree. Higher education, in my family, was not an unspoken finish. My daddy was a Georgia farm-boy with an eighth-grade education, yet it was important to him that I realize my full potential in every area of life, especially education. This, I suspect is why he began purchasing Harvard Classics for me when I was a newborn! Somehow he managed to buy the entire set. I still have it as well as the original receipt from March of 1970!

I realized, just as my entrepreneurial dream never subsided, my dream of finishing college also remained alive. As my kids grew older, I chipped away at an AA degree. I was to make sure this did not affect my kids' routines or time with me, so I never began schoolwork until they were in bed. Sometimes, I would still be working when the sun came up! Those were crazy days, but I loved them. I finished with a 4.0+ GPA and applied at The University of Texas in Austin. Two of my three children were with me when I was accepted into UT. They were proud, and I was proud to be a positive role model. I was thirty-seven years old and about to embark on another new and exciting life chapter. Aside from raising my children, those days I spent on campus at UT were *the best* days of my life. HOOK 'EM HORNS!

Food for thought: sacrifice is inevitable, but it's never too late to revisit a dream and make sure it comes true! You'll probably even inspire someone along the way.

As president of the Overachiever's Club, I earned three degrees, was hired for my first 'big girl job' in twenty years, *and* I started my freelance business, Green Pen Editing! I was also dating a great guy. Good things were happening, but bad things were also happening. While at UT, one of my best friend's sons was killed in a car accident. Sweet Garrett. He was my middle child's best friend. It was our first brush with how quick and tragic loss can create absolute heartbreak and devastation. My life perspective was forever changed. I spent the next year trying to support my daughter through this devastating loss; not to mention taking care of my son; supporting Garrett's mama (my dear friend); completing schoolwork, and taking care of myself in the process! No mother is ever prepared to see her child in such pain, and there is no remedy.

Food for thought: priorities.

The following year, my estranged adopted brother died suddenly. He *was* the chaos that I previously mentioned being raised in. So much chaos and hurt came out of his addiction and abuse that no one wanted anything to do with him. I was left with the task of communicating with the medical examiner in Florida and approving his 'pauper burial'. What a tragic way to leave this world. Another loss.

Two years later, I lost my daddy. Loss had become an ugly, uncomfortable, and unwanted theme in my life. In keeping with this unwelcomed motif, my longtime close friend, Marci, was diagnosed with stage IV ovarian cancer. She and I lost touch for a bit, but after her diagnosis, I was welcomed back into the family and jumped in as a loving and an active member of Team Marci. The next eleven months were dedicated to doing very little work, but spending as much time with her as possible. This included silliness, lots of laughing, movies, sushi, and the acclaimed Austin Film Festival (Marci's favorite). Unfortunately, these moments also included needles, scans, long drives to clinical trials, emergency hospital stays, tears, and sadly, organizing her hospice stay and palliative care. She died at home surrounded by her loving and devoted family. This experience was one of the most tragically beautiful that I have ever had.

Food for thought: no matter how busy or successful you become, make time for sweet, fun, and memorable moments with loved ones. In an instant, your world could be shattered by their absence.

During these years, I became engaged to the 'great guy', and my son and I were living with this fella (on a related note: my son and his father were estranged for about ten years). My fiancé truly was a wonderful, smart, professional man…when he was sober. I spent many years questioning whether I had committed to marrying an alcoholic. Indeed, it was true; he was an alcoholic (professionally diagnosed, but never self-admitting). My epiphany on this topic occurred while I was editing a client's manuscript! Part of the author's story was about years of living as the wife of an alcoholic. I connected with so much of her narrative that it made me realize I was in the same situation. After many years of counseling; enduring emotional abuse, and hoping for the best - I had to accept that he was not going to change. I no longer wanted to be the poster-child of codependency. I left.

Another loss. Not a 'death-loss', but still a big loss.

I also lost three fur-babies during this time. My Great Dane (Piper) suddenly dropped dead the very day I moved my belongings out of my fiancé's house. #notajoke

Food for thought: lessons and epiphanies will come from the unlikeliest of places (my client's manuscript). Keep your eyes, ears, and heart open. Even when Team Grief is kicking your ass, keep fighting.

At this point, I've got my kids, entrepreneurial spirit, degrees, a 'big girl' job, my freelance biz, and I'm in my second year of a fun and sassy single-life. All seems to be going well. My son and his dad had recently reconnected, and I had spent the last few holidays alone. I was ok with this because I was pleased that my kids were reconnecting with their dad.

On Friday, November 25, 2016, after having spent Thanksgiving with his dad, my son Conner was driving back home. I was obsessively cleaning, which is unlike me. I'm not a slob, but it was a beautiful day, and I much prefer being outside sipping a latte and reading. But this day, I was cleaning as if it were the only thing in the world I should be doing! I was scrubbing, wiping, and dusting. Nesting it seemed. Finally, around 8:30 pm, I thought, *Damn, this place is immaculate. I'm going to see a movie!* My search for movie titles and times was interrupted by a text message from my oldest daughter in Colorado Springs. The message was to her sister and me. It read, 'Somebody needs to call me now!' I called her. I could hear the fear and urgency in her voice. She said, "MOM. HAVE YOU TALKED TO DAD?" I said, "No. What?" Her voice cracked, "Mom. There was an accident. Conner didn't make it!"

I dropped the phone and then fell to my knees.

Conner didn't make it. Conner didn't make it. That's all I could hear. It bounced around in my head. *Conner didn't make it. Conner didn't make it.* My son. My baby. Is this a nightmare? *Conner didn't make it.* I need to wake up.

At that moment: Friday, 9:33 pm the day after 'Thanksgiving'. my life, my world, my heart changed forever. My twenty-two-year-old talented, intelligent and compassionate Conner; my only son - my youngest child - was gone.

Conner: self-taught musician. Talent. Self-taught programmer. Intellect. The week before he died, one of his friends said, "Hey wanna go on a nineteen-mile charity bike ride with me tomorrow?" Of course, Conner said, "Sure." Compassion. He was accepted into an advanced programmer's certification based on the knowledge he gained on his own. Before he even finished that program, he landed an incredible job developing software for The University of Texas at Austin, Center for space research. He was truly the most astonishing combination of talent, intellect, and compassion. Oh, he also spoke Japanese, studied Eastern culture, and was constantly in search of ways to be a better human. I am proud to be his mother.

Where do we go from here? There is nothing like the shattered heart of a mother, and the reality is that every moment of my life is now, and will forever be, punctuated by the loss of my son – even happy moments. It is absolute and pure devastation, and it's not a challenge that one can 'overcome'. I've spent the last year trying to stay upright in the wake of my loss - questioning my path, and being supported by my co-workers, neighbors, friends, and family.

Things you should know about me: I'm still the same person who edits your manuscript, technical manual, and court memorandums. I'm the same person who gives you honest feedback on your article. I'm the same person who procures cover-art, ISBNs, and barcodes for your book. I still own and run a successful business. I'm the same person whose entrepreneurial spirit was lit when she was twelve. I'm still a loving mother, and I still have three children. *I am myself, only different now, with all of this grief.*

I have allowed grief to guide me, and I have officially repurposed my life. In the face of tragedy and loss, I have constructed a new life out of my writing and editing skills, book publishing know how, and deep grief. This new building is held together by my son's name – by his memory and legacy – and done so in an effort to help others write, publish, and share their own stories.

I am a badass mompreneur, taking care of business, helping others, and spreading so much Conner Bovee love along the way.

Lessons Learned and Mindset Tips

Lessons learned:

1. Connect with people. Share knowledge of what you do and ask for what you need or want. People love to help.

2. Clarity, organization and setting priorities in a journal are key. It is honoring yourself, your client and your business.

3. If you take on a business partner, be clear about respective roles, goals, and responsibilities by having a proper business contract in place.

Mindset tips:

1. One must be honest and integral, in business and in life – with others and most importantly, yourself.

2. Offer integral products and services which surpasses customer satisfaction, this will lead to loyalty from your community.

3. Having a positive mindset will take you to the highest places in your life.

Aha Moments and Self Reflections

Note your Thoughts

Sarina Agi Breen

Sarina Breen is a mom of four, a wife, an entrepreneur and internet marketer who works with other entrepreneurs to help them to realize their vision and purpose.

She believes that finding your best you is always possible. With hard work and guidance from the right sources, the journey to self-discovery involves figuring out what your true passion is and realizing it.

Sarina has built several businesses both online and offline. As a former successful salon owner, she knows the value of hard work, loyalty, and customer service. However, Sarina saw the true value in moving forward in the online arena; therefore, she is currently concentrating on her digital business. She has built a successful network marketing team and has created a brand for herself in the internet marketing arena.

Sarina continues to hone her skills as a professional by investing in herself. She holds a Bachelor's Degree in Education from Temple University.

Find Sarina online:

Websites: Bit.ly/lifewithsarinabreen
http://sarinabreen.com/
Facebook: https://m.facebook.com/sarina.breen

Chapter 4

A True Intent and Purpose

By Sarina Agi Breen

'Fast forward to…' That always seemed to be what I would say when I was presenting in front of a group of people. I was always fast forwarding from one part of my life to another and forgetting about the in between.

Over the past couple of years, as I've done some serious mind-blowing soul searching, I've come to realize how important the in between stuff is. It's a part of your story, a part of your growth, a part of your journey, and an integral piece of the growth that never would have happened had it not, well…happened.

Once upon a time, I had two kids, and I wanted a third. Then I got pregnant with twins. Finding out that we were having multiples was one of those WTF moments. I guess the tiebreaker kid wanted to play dirty and give me a run for my money. I'm short; there's no room in my torso. That equals bed rest for seventeen weeks, a very unpleasant experience for my family. I already had a cute little boy who was three (Gavin), and a precious baby girl (Sydney), who was nineteen months. My husband is an amazingly patient and incredible saint of a man who dealt with it all like a champ - feeding me and taking care of two toddlers. I am going to give him a HUGE shout out right here. I LOVE YOU JOHN BREEN!

On August 16th, 2010, our twins were born. Our family was now complete. The only problem was that our baby boy Johnny looked a little off to me. I had been under the influence while having a C-section, so everyone brushed me off. But a few of my family members noticed too. He looked a little bit 'blueish'. The nurses assured us that he was fine. The docs assured me he was fine. So, five days later we went home. Five days after our trek home, when Johnny wasn't really eating or wetting his diapers - this crazy mom decided it was time to take action and call the doctor, again.

"Let's just be safe," the doc said, "take him to the local hospital and get him evaluated and we will see what they say." My husband took him to the nearest ER, and that was the beginning of a nightmare.

John called me about thirty minutes later. "Get over here," he said. "Call my dad and get over here. My mom will watch the other kids." I rushed over to be met by a horrific scene. There were about six people in the room with my baby. Nobody knew what was wrong. He was dying.

They called the local children's hospital. They called a priest. They roped off the ER area with caution tape. Within minutes, the priest was there to baptize him, and since I'm not a Catholic, I had no idea what that meant. When my husband explained it to me, I wanted to die. I wanted the earth to open up and to swallow me whole. I ran screaming down the hall. I wanted to rewind time and understand how this could happen.

Ambulances arrived from the Children's Hospital of Philadelphia with a doctor on board. We were informed that the chances of him surviving the eleven-minute ride to the hospital were slim to none. By this time, there were twenty-five people in the tiny room.

A helicopter was called in – that was his only chance of survival. Still, nobody knew what was wrong with him. He was getting no oxygen to any part of his body. He was literally suffocating. The chopper came, and they told me they would try to figure out which unit to put him on if he survived the short six-minute flight.

We kissed our baby goodbye as they placed him into a plastic bubble and we got into our car to follow the chopper to the hospital.

The ride down to the hospital was excruciating and torturous. All I could think was that our baby was gone. I screamed and cried the whole way. I don't know how John drove. Once we got there, we were directed to the cardiac floor.

Johnny had made it. He was alive – barely - but being taken care of. He had something called a coarctation of the aorta - a congenital heart defect that causes pinches the aorta and cuts off blood flow to the body.

Two days later, he had surgery to remove the bad section of his aorta, and he was on the road to recovery.

We were in the hospital for many months. After the surgery, complications arose with swallowing. Johnny ended up with a g-tube and several other complications that required surgeries that will affect him for the rest of his life.

I spent the majority of time in the hospital with him. My other children, Gavin, Sydney, and Jemma, all took it pretty hard. John stayed over as much as he could, but with his full-time job and bringing in the benefits - I took the brunt of the responsibility of the hospital stays and medical care.

It was an exhausting and stressful time for our family, to say the least. There was, however, an exciting time of happiness during all of this madness. My younger sister and only sibling was getting married!

As the day approached, we became more excited. Plans were made, dresses were picked, and showers were thrown. At ten weeks old, Johnny was able to come home to attend the ceremony with the rest of the children. Jemma, his twin, looked breathtaking in her tiny gown. It was a dream come true. My sister Helana beamed as a beautiful bride.

She had her dream wedding and married her prince charming. The next day they left for their honeymoon to Disney World in Orlando Florida.

On the airplane, there were complications. My sister didn't feel well, and she passed out. They performed CPR, and they were able to revive her heart, but her brain never recovered from the incident. Our family flew to Florida to say our goodbyes, and we pulled the life support.

There was nothing left of me. I was a shell and could no longer function. My body became weaker, and I collapsed into my own self. I was soon diagnosed with depression, and from stress, autoimmune issues flared. I was diagnosed with lupus, pseudo tumor cerebri, clotting disorders, myasthenia gravis...the list goes on. I almost died, literally.

I was a salon owner at the time. My work kept me occupied, but I was spiraling out of control. I felt that I had no focus or purpose. The only thing I could cling to was my husband and my children, but they were going through the same thing. I felt that I had nothing left. I was living for my kids - that was it. I don't remember much of that time of my life. There are chunks that are missing from my memory.

My poor Johnny was in and out of the hospital, and Jemma was being raised by grandparents, aunts, and wonderful friends - not her mommy. Gavin and Sydney were confused and sad, wondering why I was in my own world and never around. My three-year-old son told me he didn't want to be alive anymore. He was so sad – it was heart-wrenching.

As I muddled through the days, I looked for things to occupy me to keep me from thinking too much. Nothing made me happy. Somehow, a few years into my lack of consciousness, I fell upon a friend with an interesting business. When I discussed it with her, and I realized it was network marketing, I shut down. I had tried it before, but honestly, it had just been for the discount. I had never taken it seriously. I did like the products, though. I looked pretty haggard, so seeing that the products helped with appearance, I decided to give it a go with half of my heart. I found that throwing myself into something was an amazing distraction. It was a wonderful feeling to get out of a dark place and into a place of some normalcy.

I found myself putting a ton of effort into building a stable foundation in a network marketing business. I was focusing on my future and became a part of a new world where nobody seemed sad. Everyone was upbeat, positive, and super supportive. It took me away from my problems. It removed me from my sadness and made me focus on what was possible and what good I could bring rather than the bad. I started to come back out of my shell…Where would this take me? Would this take me out of my slump? I was coachable and ready to open my mind to something new - I was sick of wallowing in my own misery. So that's what I did. I built, and I learned, and I built some more. I spoke, and I grew, I planned, and I made friends. It was so empowering. I never knew that I had it in me to be a person that could build something from the ground up.

A few years into my building, I felt like something was missing. I loved the products that brought me out of my dark world; I loved my friends, and I loved my team - but something inside me was screaming. This was no longer a distraction. I felt this urge to do more. I felt like I had gone through so many trials and I was put here for a bigger purpose. I needed to get out there and help other people see their true purpose. I didn't know what my calling was yet, but I began doing some hard-core soul searching - only to discover things about myself that I never knew.

I embarked on a new journey- I sold my salon. I learned the true art of strategic marketing; but I also learned how to find out who I was as a person by ridding myself of my past demons. I have found that this comes as no easy task. It is a journey of self-discovery that never ends.

Finding yourself and passing along your knowledge of being enough is just plain hard sometimes, especially at the beginning. Self-doubt creeps in, and you think to yourself, *Who am I to be doing this, teaching this, or feeling this?* The reality is that most of us have no idea what we have inside that makes us special because we refuse to embrace it.

On your journey of self-discovery and self-worth, people will push you down. People will talk about you. Sometimes the people closest to you may think that you have gone completely out of your mind. That is ok. Keep going. Find your tribe and stick to that tribe with all your might. That is part of the process. There were so many times when I wanted to quit and stay in my room and hide.

I will tell you this. With every huge breakdown comes a huge breakthrough. That is a fact. A wall comes down, and barriers are smashed. You may not see it at this very moment, but you will emerge stronger than you were before.

We are all special, and have something inside of us that others needs to hear - sometimes it's just because it allows us feel connected to others. And sometimes because it helps others feel better about their own situation, and sometimes - a lot of times actually - you have stuff inside you to share that will positively impact others to make their own lives better.

Through this journey with my incredible tribe and my amazing mentor (who I owe so much to), I am consistently changing and bettering myself. If there is one thing that I can share as a mom who is also an entrepreneurial spirited person - it is to find your passion and your purpose. It may change as you grow, but find it and grab it – NOW. The last thing you want to do is look back on your life and remember dreams and goals that were unfulfilled due to complacency.

Too often, we focus on our end game - our result. We come into our businesses and mentorship focusing on how much we will make and our end goals. What I have come to realize is that we need to focus on our intent first. What is the true intent for doing what we are doing? And is it a true intent and purpose? Can we get out of bed in the morning clinging to that intent when the world is looming and wants to push us back down? Once we figure out that true intent driving us forward, only then can we truly enjoy the journey.

Enjoying the journey is a great saying. We say it all the time. We see cute Canva quotes that tell us to love our life and enjoy the journey. But do we? Do we really? Do we celebrate the small wins every day along the way - or do we just hope for the next big thing? One thing that I will tell you is that along my journey, I forgot to celebrate for a really long time. I would concentrate so hard on what was next, or what I needed to do to make a certain amount of money, that I forgot to celebrate and enjoy each step of the way.

Each step is an important piece of your journey and your puzzle. You need those pieces to become the person that you are. I needed each and every skinned knee and every disappointment and small win along the way to see what is truly possible for myself. My best advice is to never discount each day and what it means. Each day is a learning experience, and if you use each day to its fullest potential - and heck - even if you don't, count it as a win because you are trying to be just a little bit better than you were the day before.

My story doesn't end here. Not by a mile. It's just beginning. I know for sure that I have a lot to learn about not only the world around me, but the true nature of myself and others. Our demons and our past, as well as the daunting fear of future may lurk; but it is our duty as moms, wives, partners, entrepreneurs, daughters, or whoever we may be, to rise up from the old to create a new vision of ourselves. One that is grander, more beautiful, and more amazing than you could have ever imagined. You have a responsibility to shine your light in this world, and to bring your beauty upon it - and to let them all know that you have arrived. No more hiding. You are fierce. You are driven. You are confident. You are beautiful. You are you.

Lessons Learned and Mindset Tips

Lessons learned:

1. When you want to quit, don't. You will regret it.

2. When everyone tells you that you can't. You can. I promise. It's really, really hard, but you can do it and don't let ANYONE stop you.

3. Your journey is greater than your outcome. Live your life in abundance, serve others, put good out into the world, and enjoy each small step as you take it. The universe will pour greatness into you as you pour greatness into the universe.

Mindset tips:

1. Always know that what you have to say is valuable and important. There is always someone out there that is waiting to hear what you have to say.

2. You are an exceptional human being. You are enough, you are strong, and you are you. No matter what anyone thinks or says, nobody can ever take your unique qualities away from you, and that is what makes you special and amazing.

3. When you have reached your goal, don't get complacent. Look at yourself and your life. Rethink your goals and your strategies. Once you've done that, create a new and grander, bigger, and more incredible vision of yourself than you'd ever thought possible. If you can truly manifest it and believe it, you can make it happen.

Aha Moments and Self Reflections

Note your Thoughts

Jenna Carelli

Jenna Carelli (as seen on NBC, FOX, ABC, and CBS) is a mom fueled by coffee, wine, and whiskey. Jenna's mission is to serve wellness professionals and authors in a way that is authentic to themselves and their brand. Jenna's company is a team of professionals who have made money in their own businesses. They work within their own zone of genius, to allow you to scale your business and automate it completely so that your time is free and you are available to focus more on yourself and your family. Jenna's team provides high-level business strategy and full-service implementation so that you can work less, yet earn a lot more. Her team thrives on giving their clients a business and lifestyle that they are freaking obsessed with!

Find Jenna online:

Website: http://www.jennacarelli.com
Facebook: http://www.facebook.com/jcarelliconsulting
Instagram: http://www.instagram.com/jennacarelli

Chapter 5

Mindset over the Middle Row

By Jenna Carelli

We invited her on our week-long family vacation without a doubt in our minds. In a matter of days, we decided she'd never receive an invite to a family trip again...ever.

I had a thought at the forefront of my mind that day. There was something telling me to just let it out - tell the world! I decided to go for it. I told everyone from the backseat of our fourteen-passenger van that I wanted to be an entrepreneur. I was going to quit my job as a corporate paralegal and pursue a job as a personal trainer and nutrition coach.

Almost immediately, I caught the attention of a fellow entrepreneur in the car who was very intrigued, asking all the nitty-gritty details of a start-up entrepreneur. Then, BOOM! The moment happened.

A voice came from the middle aisle. She told me I'd never be successful if I quit my corporate job. "I have always had a dream of starting a bed and breakfast, but I'll never pursue that dream because dreams don't come true," she said. This person later went on to tell me that the man of my dreams would never marry me if I became self-employed. She said that I wouldn't be able to provide for a family if I was in business for myself.

So there I sat; a visionary with a solid dream. A dream that was completely shattered with words (and even worse, through expression) in a matter of seconds.

I had finally built up the courage to share this vision with those who I felt were closest to me, and I was shut down. I cried. I balled my eyes out right there in the back seat of that passenger van.

I could have taken this toxic encounter and brushed it off as one person's viewpoint. Certainly one person does not have the power to dictate my future. Except, I've always been a people-pleaser. I've always wanted everyone to like me. I'm the person who says sorry without reason when someone else isn't paying attention and accidentally bumps into me on the street.

I let this one toxic encounter rule the next year of my life.

The power of one interaction can set the tone for the days, months, or years thereafter if you let it! Remember the old adage, 'Sticks and stones may break my bones, but words will never hurt me'. For the first twenty-seven years of my life, that phrase never spoke true to me. Negative words didn't just harm me; they injured me emotionally. I would later come to recognize this cycle of conflict, acknowledge that it starts from within, and learn how to manage it before it amounted to anything serious. However, at the moment, and for the next several months following this encounter, I handled things a bit differently.

When she shot down my dream, I was initially surprised; I didn't quite understand why anyone would be so dismissive of someone else's dream. Then I was angry, so angry with this one particular individual. Then, in a matter of seconds, I was terrified. I internalized every piece of that day, every word that was said. I started believing that I was foolish, selfish, and dumb for having dreams. It took me a year to figure out how to manage this toxic relationship, and then I had to take action to piece my life back together. It's one thing to come to a realization and acknowledge it, but it's a totally separate ball-game (and one that many don't play) to actually take action and execute. Here's how my toxic encounter with one person spiraled into a series of complications in other areas of my life.

It added trouble, difficulty, hardship, and distress to many of my relationships moving forward. I once looked up to this particular adult, who then told me I would be worthless if I pursued my dream. I was left with emotional scars, and it seemed like they multiplied by the day. Then I started to question the relationships I had with friends and even my boyfriend at the time.

I started experiencing social anxiety, always feeling as though I was in survival mode and needed to prove everyone wrong. I had to work on troubleshooting relationships. I had to learn how to truly manage and cope with a judgmental/hypercritical society. I recognized that I was focusing on survival and getting through my own struggles and completely forgetting about feeding other relationships that were important to me.

I started hating myself even more, and began to align my self-worth with other judgmental friends and their comments. I became unaligned with the person who I truly was and the person who I wanted to be. I became submissive to my own arbitrary thoughts.

Despite feeling as though all odds were against me, I persevered hard towards my entrepreneurial dreams. I took baby steps and followed through on every gut feeling, every notion of my intuition. I would work on my business in the early morning and late evening hours, and in between those hours, I would go through the motions of my day job as a corporate paralegal.

During this time, I learned to accept the fact that this person was not going to give me her blessing. I learned how to stand up for what I believed in and to stop seeking approval from everyone else. I learned how to stop being so apprehensive that I was making the wrong decisions and would have to apologize for my actions. I was annoyed when I learned that this person wasn't the only one with this viewpoint - that it was actually a quite popular societal belief that entrepreneurship is a recipe for disaster. I learned to trust that I had the ability to carve my own path and was capable of believing in myself, trusting my intuition and gut.

Initially, my goal was to prove ONE person wrong. However, this was a petty and extremely selfish goal. I dug a really deep hole and took a highly toxic relationship that already stuck like glue, and added super-glue to the mix. It turns out that it is not healthy trying to prove one person wrong for any length of time. After all, I had dreams of changing the world - who cares about one person!? A few short months later, I married the man of my dreams. Then, BOOM, the mindset shift happened.

The mindset shift was the extra fuel I needed to kick things into high gear in my business and make things happen. It was a direct result of an outside motivational factor (one that ironically, happened to be inside me at the time).

I found out that I was pregnant and discovered a piece of self-love by way of growing a tiny human. Mama-mode kicked in pretty quickly. Everything shifted; my mindset, my outlook, and my career path. I gave myself a corporate exit strategy: nine months to, at a minimum, match my monthly corporate salary so I could quit my unfulfilling job and stay home with my beautiful daughter. It's funny how such a strong force of motivation like finding out you are pregnant makes you realize just how overworked, underpaid, and unrewarding your current job really is.

It was go-time. Instead of just believing in myself and knowing that I could do it, I now had to take those thoughts and beliefs and put them into action. The risk of staying in my corporate job and not getting to watch my little girl grow up was great enough now.

I built a six-figure business after the mindset shift. All while raising a newborn, working less and going against every single thing that society told me to do. I am here to tell you that you can do it too. No matter what your story is or what part of your journey you are currently in.

Here's why.

You are powerful. So powerful that you have the ability to wipe out all other conflicts in your life. All you need to do is seek to love yourself more, and avoid aligning your self-worth with the approval of others. I have admiration for myself, along with joy and love for those closest to me more than ever before. It will always be a work-in-progress kind of love and admiration, but when you can see yourself for who you truly are (and not what others may or may not think of you), nothing else matters. This didn't start happening for me until the mindset shift. What matters most is asking yourself, "Am I going to take action on this dream, this passion, or am I going to sit around and let it drag me down day-in and day-out?" I hope your answer is action. Action is fulfilling.

I am now in the business of teaching others to follow their dreams, make their passion a reality, and do it in a way that frees up their time, so they have energy to give to their loved ones. My mission is to serve entrepreneurs in a way that is authentic to themselves and their brand. I want you to 'go for it!' and 'beat the odds'. Seek to love yourself more and forget about the approval of others. This will lead to never-ending optimism, buoyancy, positivity, and tenacity that will shine through to every person you encounter.

It's time to make the switch from dream-mode to action-mode. I chose to make the switch when I found out I was pregnant with my daughter. This might mean taking a huge risk on yourself and your family for a greater return. Or it could mean taking baby steps and tackling one item at a time. For me, this meant signing-off on a steady paycheck with good health benefits and setting aside my personal hobbies and selfishness for a little while, to create something bigger and better for my family. I took a series of small steps to address my challenges and adversity. It didn't happen overnight, and it wasn't a spontaneous decision. It was hard work. I needed to swallow my pride for a bit and recognize my own internal struggles with the fear of not being good enough, smart enough, savvy enough, or educated enough to stand in my own power and say yes to something that had been nudging me for a long time.

So many of us are afraid to take the next step; we are fearful of doing something outside the norm of what society teaches us to do, or too afraid of what someone else might think of our decisions, rather than narrowing in on our own personal happiness and future expectations.

I am the daughter of an entrepreneur. I watched my father run his own business, dictate his own hours, and call the shots in his own life. I was introduced to self-employment at a young age, yet I went to school with doctors' children. When I was in grade school, I felt the societal pull to grow up and have a job with all kinds of letters behind my name. After the mindset shift, I set a new mission for my business and myself: to impact a larger part of this world in a way that truly feels good, get rid of friendships that instigated negative behavior, stand in my own power and speak my mind freely.

Find your mindset shift and become the powerful person you are meant to be.

Lessons Learned and Mindset Tips

Lessons learned:

1. Work on yourself first. When you shift into the entrepreneurial space, there is this continual effort of needing to dig deep into figuring out the essence of what your passion and purpose is and how you'll continue to find yourself deserving of this new reality. It is important to really understand what your passion is, what drives you, why you are in business for yourself, and why you do the things that you do. Really hone in on who you truly are. When you are in your zone with your blinders on and creating original content, that is when you rise above the rest.

2. Don't add to the white noise in the digital space. Bring out that one unique factor about yourself that makes you stand out in this space. You are creating your business from your heart, your mind, and your life experiences. Don't allow yourself to be dissatisfied due to comparison.

3. Take time to learn how to be present, and more charismatic. Pay attention to what is going on rather than being caught up in your own thoughts. Listen to your audience and be pro-active in solving their pain-points. When you are present, your audience will feel listened to, respected, and valued.

Mindset tips:

1. Don't stop writing and journaling. Get your true feelings and emotions down on paper. Solidify those thoughts in your head before society has a chance to persuade them.

2. Share these feelings and emotions. If you aren't quite ready to share your words with another human being or audience, simply re-read them to yourself. The act of transferring

ownership of your inner thoughts from your head to a piece of paper or online journal is very therapeutic. It reduces the feelings of anxiety, uncertainty, and dissatisfaction.

3. Intertwine your story with your message. Use your story whether good, bad or ugly, to communicate, connect and resonate with your audience.

Aha Moments and Self Reflections

Note your Thoughts

_____

_____

_____

_____

_____

_____

_____

_____

_____

_____

_____

_____

_____

_____

_____

_____

_____

_____

_____

_____

Meagan Fettes

Meagan Fettes is a proud and active mama to two young boys. She runs a successful business teaching yoga and facilitates yoga teacher training and retreats around the world. Meagan also offers one-on-one coaching and healing sessions. She is a certified holistic master coach, Reiki level ½, and a higher priestess practitioner level ½.

Meagan is currently building a tipi retreat center in DeWinton, Alberta with her family. Her journey has been challenging; she struggled with abuse and addiction before landing on the path of healing, entrepreneurship, and motherhood. She is grateful for the opportunities of growth she has been given as they have truly opened her ability to divinely guide thousands of people onto their own path of healing and empowerment. Meagan shares a lot of passion and love through her work and looks forward to sharing the depths of her story to support the growth of more people.

Find Meagan online:

Website: www.meagan-fettes.com
Facebook: www.facebook.com/meaganfettescoaching

Chapter 6

The Art of Letting Go

By Meagan Fettes

I remember the day I had my oldest son. I was so in love with this human being, but I was also full of fear and excitement at the same time. I never knew I could experience so many emotions at once. The morning I had him, I stared at him for hours, in complete awe in every way. His hands so little, yet larger than I could have imagined before seeing him. The perfect form of his face and the beautiful contours of his lips. Even the sound of his whimpers and cries brought this feeling of expansion within my heart. There was no way I could sleep. There I sat, my life changed forever, unable to process the emotions I felt. I was so proud to be in the hospital holding my son…my son, even that idea of having a child still felt foreign to me, yet also comfortable. I spent the rest of the early morning hours attempting to learn how to breastfeed. I sat in silence watching the city lights from my hospital bed. I didn't want to put him down, but in the back of my mind ran the ongoing tape of the entrepreneurial to-do list I had to tackle.

As the sun began to rise, I laid my son down and replaced him with my laptop, emailing away, tackling the to-do list, while my husband slept soundly in the hospital bed. One of the nurses came in and laughed at the scene; I'm sure it looked quite interesting. "Meagan, you just had a baby. Remember, you need to rest when the baby rests," she said before leaving the room. I knew that. I often heard that statement in the final weeks of my pregnancy. Rest when the baby rests. I believed that the person who originally said that had never run a business. At that time, I had been on the road to being an entrepreneur for many years already, but the idea of being a mom was totally new to me.

During the first six months of being a mom, I resisted the demands and attempted to remain a part-time mother and a full-time business owner. The only challenge was, the 'boss' of my 'part-time' mom job was a bit more demanding than I had originally anticipated. They were, by far, the most challenging months I have ever experienced. My son was colicky, so at a week and a half old and he woke up out of the so-called sleepy newborn stage and began testing out his voice. I tried everything I could to console him. We drove for hours, and he spent time in his baby swing. I spent most of our days bouncing from one idea to the next, hoping that something would calm him down long enough for me to calm down as well. Some days he cried for as long as twelve hours. Finally, one day, I was done, and my emotions were right on the surface. My husband and I fought and struggled to maintain a relationship, blaming each other constantly for the challenges we were experiencing as parents. Due to the communication and hostility in our relationship, we spent more time apart. I sat feeling completely alone, sinking into the depths of despair. I felt completely lost and trapped, with no direction of how to move forward. I called my mom, hoping she would give me a quick fix to try, as moms always know what to do. She reassured me I was not a bad mother, and told me to strap him into the stroller and walk laps around the Quonset of our property. I walked, and I cried. The tears I cried were not the ones of joy I had been promised in the brochure. I realized that not only were my son and I suffering, my business also was unsuccessful, and my marriage was on the rocks. Nothing seemed to be working, no matter how few hours I slept or how hard I worked.

Have you ever had one of those breakdown moments? The moments where you fall to your knees, raise the white flag and surrender to life. I've had a couple. One specifically where I finally chose to make some changes and put my family, my son, and myself first above all. Now for some, this may seem like an obvious immediate choice when you have a baby. I told myself I had been on my journey as an entrepreneur since the age of twenty-two. I felt called to share my passions and my gifts of healing with the world, so when I got pregnant at the age of twenty-six with my oldest son, I struggled with the idea of putting my business on the sidelines. At first, as I journeyed through my own healing, I associated with the value I placed upon myself while I built my business or the achievement I felt when I grew as an entrepreneur. As I worked into myself a bit further, I realized that it wasn't that at all...I was afraid. I was afraid to fail at the one job I felt completely uncertain in, the one job I truly saw the most value in – being a mother. I felt unworthy to play such a crucial role in this being's life.

Most of the fear came from the workings of my past. I spent many years addicted to drugs and alcohol. Despite growing up in a loving and supportive home, I learned to escape my feelings of shame and guilt from sexual and physical abuse from old relationships through numbing my emotions by getting high and wasted. Even though I had been clean for a few years before getting pregnant with my son and believing I had embarked on my healing journey, I still held onto the idea that I could not successfully raise a child with the shame of my past. Instead of dealing with the emotions as they arose, I moved from my addiction to cocaine and alcohol to working endless hours on my business, and justified it as it was a healthier choice at the time. The state of being busy to avoid the true healing that needed to take place.

The funny thing about having kids is that they emulate your emotions ten-fold. They truly are the best teachers we could ask for on this spiritual journey. When my oldest son was six months old, a friend gave me a book, The Conscious Parent, and told me to read it due to some behaviors he was showing. At first, I was a bit taken aback, dropping deeper into the depths of guilt of failing as a mother. I went home and read it cover to cover in just two sittings. It resonated to me. The words on each page made everything I was experiencing clear, and I knew exactly what I needed to do. What I took from it was the idea that when a child is displaying a behavior, it is a response to what we as parents are experiencing within. It creates an awareness of the internal workings of our minds, our hearts, and how we perceive ourselves and the world around us. This made complete sense to me.

That was a pivotal moment. I knew I had to embark on my own spiritual path to heal my heart and past wounds. I invested in training focused on healing my heart and releasing the attachment of guilt and responsibility I associated with my past, and how the deeps cuts affected my parenting. I decided to focus on my own growth over anything else, even over my business.

During this time, I got pregnant with my youngest son, and again the guilt kicked in. How could I raise another child when I still hadn't discovered how to support my first-born? I was afraid I would rebound right back into the same patterns; going through each day wishing for it to be over and wishing away what people claimed as the best part of a child's life, the early years.

I had no idea what I was going to learn or how it was going to affect my journey as a mompreneur. The focus on my personal growth drastically changed everything in my life. I focused the first part of my training on truly healing the thorns in my heart and the ideas of shame and guilt I held onto. To do that I had to get real and share my story. I shared my inner truths with people I didn't know, people who soon became my closest friends, to shed my old skin and reignite my flame. The bounds within our group were real - I had found my people. I finally felt like I had space to feel. I grew my business and set boundaries around my time. I learned how to say no to things that no longer served me, and delegated my needs of support to those around me.

The journey to healing my heart led to healing my past, the shame I held so deep, and the relationship I created with my kids. I made so many changes within the first few months of committing to this journey. I decided to drastically shift everything in my business life. I let go of the not-for-profit organization I spent years building, recognizing that the amount of resistance I had met over the years was a prime message that I was not meant to travel that road. I parted ways with my business partner. The communication we had with our last training was not supportive to either of us. We had grown in separate ways as teachers and generated different visions for how and what we wanted to teach. I had created space for myself to tap into what I wanted to generate with my skills and decided to get on a journey to developing my own training, retreats, and spiritual teachings. As strange as it may seem, the most gratifying choice was to let go of all the ideas I had held of what success looked like, and truly choose to live from my heart, sharing my stories and my gifts authentically. I also learned how to generate balance.

Self-care has become a vital piece of my day as I have learned through experience that my kids respond to my energy. If I am feeling stressed and overwhelmed, their behaviors become more challenging to deal with. My patience is non-existent it feels. I react faster and stress out over the smallest things if I don't carve out that time for myself each day to connect and support myself from my heart.

'A good mother always takes care of herself first.' This quote changed my life and my relationships with my kids, family, and business. The concept of this quote is important to thrive in life as a mompreneur.

Every morning when I wake up, I ask myself, What do I need to feel supported and loved today? Often all I need is stillness. For me, that means I wake up every morning a few hours before everyone else in my house. I spend an hour in meditation and yoga practice and may even take some time to indulge in the sweet practice of journaling. I then take the extra time to simply be, before getting organized through acting on what is essential in completing that day for business. The more organized I create my morning, the more space and time I find I have throughout the day to honor whatever comes up.

Some days I allow myself to sleep in and rest. There is no perfect formula for balance from what I have seen, other than to slow down and be intentional with how you support yourself. The support you want to give others needs to be given to yourself first and foremost so you can give from your heart. Check in with what is of the highest value for you today, what will serve you and your intentions best today?

Balance. The idea of balance is one thing, understood in the fact that it is essential to our well-being and ability to thrive and reduce stress. Implementing the word and the idea into everyday life is its own journey, one that is riddled with ups and downs. For me, balance in being a mom and an entrepreneur has come together in the most raw and organic way possible, through experiential growth and learning.

As a spiritual teacher, yoga instructor/facilitator and coach, the road to truly implementing balance in my everyday life led to my greatest breakdowns and my biggest breakthroughs. I have learned much more about myself and how to support my family, my business, and myself. I've taken a step back and let go of the image I have had in my mind of how I thought it 'should' be and am open to the multiple possibilities of what 'might' be.

The other day my youngest woke up and just held me in the tightest hug he has given me yet. When my eldest woke up, he did the same thing, hugged me tight and told me he loved me. He asked me to stay home with him and play with him. I realized that I had been out of balance, working more than giving myself space to play. I looked at my schedule and decided that I could take the day to be with my kids. To play, unwind myself, and embrace the moments of love.

Slow down and create space for yourself to be present in each moment. The reins of parenting will become simpler, and your business will flourish, as you will have time to build relationships and put effort into your projects. What does self-care mean to you? Recognize how you can make subtle changes to your perception to bring in support and self-care. Know that you are worth taking the time to connect with each day and by focusing on your growth and your self-love first, you will be able to give a lot more.

I have set work hours that I hold myself accountable to. Where I used to sit on my phone all night responding to emails and partially playing with my boys, I now take the time to put all my electronics away, turn my phone onto silent, and commit to being present with them. My eldest is in the stage of creativity. When I am fully present, listening to his words and building into his creative world he speaks with clarity and confidence, he gets excited about what we are doing, and he plays with his little brother. For the first time, I heard the two of them laughing together, thoroughly enjoying a moment of playing with a big red exercise ball, bouncing it back and forth to each other and laughing joyously with each pass. I can enjoy these moments when I take the time to honor myself first by choosing to create a balance between work, play and rest.

The key to balance is allowing yourself to always develop and grow. Myself, I am still new on my journey as a momboss. Currently, my boys are three years old and one year old. I know that my idea of balance and self-care will change as we transition to the school years, and eventually into the teenage years of sports and extracurricular activities. I'm slowing down, focusing on my own self-care and allowing what is to be. I trust my journey will continue to teach me and support me in the growth I need to be the best version, in all the different hats I wear.

Lessons Learned and Mindset Tips

Lessons learned:

1. Scale back to generate success in all areas of your life. Focus on one thing in business until you create major success within it, so that you can also support the all other areas of your life.

2. Ask for support – the key to balance is delegation. Be clear with your communication and express exactly what you need so you can support yourself and others.

3. Put your own healing and well-being first! This was the lesson that took me the longest to learn but it was the most valuable of them all. If you are not caring for yourself and taking time to receive, what you give will run you dry? A good mother always takes care of herself first. By doing that, you will fill your own cup and your children and those around you will follow your lead.

Mindset questions:

1. What is the one thing I can do in my business that will generate true results?

2. What can I do that would support my well-being and myself?

3. How can I find the time to do what nurtures me?

Remember, you are worthy and you are an amazing mama! Take it one day at a time and celebrate establishing habits that support you and all that you do.

Aha Moments and Self Reflections

Note your Thoughts

Kelli Freese

Kelli is an integrative nutritional health coach as well as a French and British aromatherapy student. She helps women with thyroid Imbalance understand what is going on with their body and helps them ease back into balance without getting overwhelmed or feeling out of control. Many of Kelli's clients have called her The Hormone Whisperer, and she strives to live up to that title so that she can have it engraved on a plaque one day. Kelli resides in Austin, TX with her incredibly supportive husband, five active kids, fluffy golden retriever, and a quiet Russian tortoise.

Find Kelli online:

Instagram: https://www.instagram.com/essentially.kelli/
Website: http://www.essentiallykelli.com/

Complimentary consultation:
https://kellifreesehealthandwellness.as.me/

Chapter 7

The Health Coach Warrior

By Kelli Freese, INHC

As I sit here and reflect on my journey into the mompreneur world, I have to smile. My daughter is next to me telling me about the ballet studio she wants to start one day, and my twins are sitting on the floor designing their dinosaur park that they plan on owning and operating. I've been told that moms that run their own business are strong and show their children that they can do anything. I've never considered myself as a fiercely independent woman or a role model for my children. In fact, I never planned on owning and operating my own business; it just sort of happened. Although I went about starting my own company in an odd way, I've made mistakes but I've learned a lot. Each mistake molded and chiseled me into the mom and woman I am and has helped define what my business is today; thriving and growing.

In 2012, I wanted a natural remedy for my baby daughter's constant digestive issues. I was prescribed baby Zantac, but it just felt wrong to give it to her. As I was talking to my 'crunchy' friends, I fell into the deep spiraling hole of essential oils and natural remedies. I was already trying to switch over to a more natural way of eating, and essential oils just seemed to fit into that lifestyle. A friend taught a class on essential oils for a few others and me. I was hooked on what they could do to help my baby and my three older boys. Then, when the kit arrived, I let them sit on my counter for a few weeks because I was unsure of what to do with them. I started doing research and slowly started using the oils. As I began to use them, I naturally started telling my friends about them, and I opened my house up for a few more classes. I had no idea that I was starting a business that would, at the time of writing this, land me in the top 0.2% of the company. I just wanted to help women that wanted natural alternatives for their kids and family. As my business grew slowly, I began to make other changes for our family. I changed the way we ate and lost seventy-five pounds. My eldest son was no longer constantly at the doctor for respiratory problems and heart palpitations. I had people referring friends to me for consults, and to be honest, I wasn't sure what to do with them!

I began researching naturopathic schools and realized that to go that route I would have to be in school for quite some time. In 2014, my husband and I decided that I should enroll in the Institute of Integrative Nutrition's Integrative Health Coaching program. I would graduate in twelve months, but be able to work with clients in six months. I loved the program, and I was overjoyed that I would have some sort of certification to make myself officially a health coach. After graduating from IIN, I felt the nudge to enroll in the Mastering Thyroid Imbalance for Health Coaches program. I didn't have thyroid issues. In fact, I didn't even know anyone with thyroid problems, but I felt in the depths of my soul that I needed to take this course. I'm so happy I did because as the course was finishing up, I found a lump in my throat exactly where the thyroid is located. After a quick visit to the doctor, I was sent off for an ultrasound, and from there, sent scrambling for a biopsy. I was told over and over that I was too healthy to have cancer. Spoiler alert, nobody is 'too healthy' for cancer.

When I woke up from surgery to have my thyroid removed, I heard a voice inside of me telling me what a fake I was. Who was I to help people to become healthier? I was a fraud. I was just some housewife with five kids trying to pretend that she had it all together. I struggled with depression. I signed up for a course and never even finished it (I'm not even sure what the course was on at this point), and felt like an even bigger loser. People reached out to tell me how strong I was. I hid behind a smile or my computer screen and acted as if I wasn't falling apart. I hired a coach to help me find balance. She sent me her workbook, and we had a few calls in which she told me what to do. I realized that this was not what I had signed up for. Then, I sat in silence and wrote. I wrote some more. Then, in that silence, I knew that I was supposed to use my journey through thyroid cancer to help other people with health struggles. I was 'lucky' in that I knew what I could do to get my meds right and choose which treatments would be best for me. So many people don't have that, and they end up frustrated and confused. I wanted to be the person that could help them emotionally, physically and nutritionally as they worked with their doctor medically. I jumped into that niche and realized that I loved it, but I struggled with it as well. I felt like a piece of my program was missing.

As I journaled and worked on defining how I would help my clients through their health issues, I realized that I had really kept my oil business and my health coaching segregated. I was embarrassed by being so high in a MLM company and did not want to seem pushy or salesy to anyone. I supported my team and held classes, but didn't really encourage my current health coaching clients to use oils. That's when it hit me, much like an anvil hitting the Roadrunner. I needed to combine everything. I didn't care if my clients were current oil users or not, it wasn't about getting them enrolled on my team, it was about helping people and improving their life.

After combining all of my niches and passions I started talking to my doctor, they had been working with me for two years, so they had seen my progress and knew my story. I set up a referral partnership with them, along with a midwife and a few chiropractors that I knew and trusted. By building relationships with these businesses first, it was comfortable to flow into a referral partnership because we already respected each other.

As my company began to thrive, I began to struggle. I was tired, gaining weight and struggling emotionally. My husband and I took stock of our lives and realized that I was not taking the time for myself that I needed to. To start, I decided that moving my body was vital to my health and those around me. I joined a 9Round Kickboxing gym that was close to my house. Then I set up a schedule for my online time as well as boundaries around my work time. By having a structured start and end to my workday, I was no longer up until all hours of the night working. I also structured family time. With five kids that my husband and I homeschool it can be really easy to overschedule our days and weeks. That wasn't something that we wanted, so we carve out time that we can go and have fun. I also shut down all electronics by nine. To be real here, there are days that I break this rule, and I always feel it the next day because my sleep isn't as good on those nights. I also started hiring help. This was a hard thing for me because I am so incredibly vested in how I want things to be done. However, there are certain things I must have help with. For instance, anything tech-oriented takes me so long to do, but a virtual assistant can complete these tasks in five minutes. It made sense to hire some help, and in doing so, it saved my sanity.

I also hired a business and life coach to help me balance everything and assist me in growing even more. I invested a TON of money, as in thousands, and as I worked through her program and tried to set up her systems, it felt like sticking a round peg in a square hole. I became frustrated and spent a lot of time feeling irritated with this coach. I had heard amazing things about her, and so obviously she was going to be a miracle worker for me, I was bound to be able to 'hit the next level' after working with her! Then, reality hit. I was trying to become this coach, and that wasn't me. I wasn't being authentic, so I was never going to grow. I learned once again to trust my gut and follow my instincts. I decided that working with a business coach wasn't what I needed to be doing at that time, so I decided to not renew my contract and instead see what would happen if I followed my gut 100%. For some reason following my gut was the scariest thing I've ever had to do, it was even scarier than having a homebirth with my fifth child. Then, I got an email that I knew I had to jump on.

An amazing business coach and friend of mine was forming a beta Mizmind group, and she wondered if I wanted in. I ended up in this group that met weekly, and we talked about what was working and what wasn't. We began following our intuition and gave each other feedback. We laughed together. We discussed life. Deep friendships were made across the US (can I just stop for a minute here and mention how much I adore Zoom), and a year and a half later we still meet to discuss business. This group was a godsend, and if I hadn't decided to listen to my gut, I would have never joined it. The best part of this group is that it was a collection of women that wanted to do things a little bit differently and we were all willing to jump in and see what happened.

I've realized that it can feel like you are constantly spinning and getting nowhere as you jump hurdles to get a business off the ground. You can feel like a fraud as everything that you have worked so hard to build falls apart. You aren't a fraud. The way that one successful entrepreneur built her business may not work for you, and that's fine. That doesn't make you any less of a success, your success will happen differently.

For me, I wasn't willing to sacrifice homeschooling my kids, date nights, and sleep to grow my business. When I was able to say no to a client because they weren't my ideal client, I felt like a success. For you, it could be hiring a housekeeper or paying cash for a trip that makes you feel successful. Celebrate that success! You were made for greatness, don't settle for less. Listen to your gut, it won't steer you wrong. Moms were given a beautiful intuition, but we have been taught that it isn't steering us correctly. Ignore that teaching, tap into your intuition and you can't go wrong. I can't wait to read your success story!

Lessons Learned and Mindset Tips

Lessons learned:

1. **You are stronger than you think.** It's easy to stay down when things go wrong. Sometimes business deals go wrong. You or a family member may get a bad doctor's report. Awful things happen, but they aren't the end of the world. It would be even more awful if you didn't get back up and keep on going. Pick your favorite fight song, an amazing quote, etc. Get it stuck in your head to keep you going.

2. **Trust your gut.** There are a million ways to make your business succeed, that's why there are a million business books on Amazon. The right way for you to make your business a success is to do what works for you. Don't get me wrong, business coaches and advisors are great, but if they are intent on doing things their way then they aren't good coaches. If they are willing to work with you and teach you to follow your gut, then they are worth their weight in gold.

3. **Balance.** Find the balance that works for you. You will never have everything perfectly proportioned, but it will be balanced enough for you. Live in that spot so that you can blossom and grow into what works for you.

Mindset tips:

1. Self-care. Schedule it in for yourself. You and your people will thank you!

2. Ask for help and be also willing to receive it.

3. Surround yourself with like-minded people to build a community.

Aha Moments and Self Reflections

Note your Thoughts

_____

_____

_____

_____

_____

_____

_____

_____

_____

_____

_____

_____

_____

_____

_____

_____

_____

_____

Traci King

Traci King is a successful traditional business owner and entrepreneur who's building an online business with a health and wellness company.

Living in Indianapolis, she and her husband of twenty years grew a multi-million-dollar business building countertops starting from their garage. Eleven years later, the business is continuing to thrive.

Traci is passionate about business and loves sharing what she's learned to help others achieve success. She believes in the power of positivity by building people up and making a positive impact through encouragement, vision, and mindset.

After overcoming a difficult knee surgery, she understands the importance of sharing her knowledge. Traci is focused on a clean living lifestyle and believes in the use of supplements to aid in healing and overall wellness by teaching and empowering others.

As a mom to a busy son, Traci enjoys attending his many activities and sports. She spends her free time with family, friends, and enjoying the outdoors. She loves to travel, especially to the beach!

Find Traci online:

Facebook: www.facebook.com/traci.lundebergking
LinkedIn: www.linkedin.com/in/traci-king-0598702

Chapter 8

The Importance of Perseverance

By Traci King

As I arrived at our company early that morning, my heart was heavy, and my head was spinning. I had no clue how we were going to get ourselves out of this mess. It was in the spring of 2008, and our business had hit some hard times. Money was tight, jobs we had under contract were delayed, and customers who still owed us money had closed their doors due to the downturn in the economy. Worst of all, we had just been informed that our biggest customer was under investigation by the government for fraud! Our customer's assets were seized, and all operations were on hold, including several open jobs we had going. Needless to say, they owed us money, a make or break amount of money.

As I walked in, I sat down with my other business partners, one of them being my husband, Robert. We reviewed the books, looked at the profit and loss margins, poured over the financial statements, and examined the backlog of jobs we had in the pipeline. We spent the next several days brainstorming on how we could develop a plan to get more business and cut costs. We even discussed looking for a buyer for the business, and last resort, closing our doors. Our line of credit was close to being maxed out and our options seemed impossible, dismal and limited. After days of intense and exhausting discussions, we concluded if we wanted to stay in business, we would have to make some very difficult choices. It seemed as if the perfect storm had hit, and it hit hard.

It was early February 2006, when we first started making countertops in our garage, an opportunity presented itself to us to build them for a general contracting company that represented a unique client. Our customer was in a pinch, and quite frankly, we needed the extra money. My husband Robert can build anything, so a few countertops was not a problem. At the time, we both worked full-time jobs, and our son Collin was about two years old. After long days of work, we would come home, eat dinner, get our son to bed, grab the baby monitor and then head out to the garage to begin working. This routine went on for several months. After the first shipment of countertops left our garage, our customer called again and wanted us to make more, a lot more, a commercial contract was under negotiation for us to build countertops for a potential sixty buildings. Before we knew it, our three-car garage was full!

As the contract for the sixty buildings was finalizing, and additional orders came in, we had to decide if we were going to continue down this path and start a business, or pass the work to an already established countertop company. I mean, at this point, we already had the customers, so why not give it a go. We leased a space, brought on another partner and started to grow our business.

Our growth was fast, within our first five years, we doubled our revenue and needed to move and expand our space. We invested several hundred thousand dollars into our business: buying equipment and tools, and hiring employees. We also added cabinet manufacturing to our business. Due to the nature of our customer's unique client, we built, shipped and installed cabinets and countertops all over the U.S. We even had a hand in creating a custom design, a unique piece of furniture that is still used in their centers today. Our business was off to a great start.

That was until the storm hit in the spring of 2008. The customer who essentially started our business was the one being investigated for fraud. I'm sure you can imagine our surprise when we received the call regarding the investigation. I sat in complete disbelief, struggling to fully understand and comprehend the conversation I was hearing.

All job sites were shut down immediately and all subcontractors in association with this company would also be subject to an audit. Funds were frozen until the investigation was completed. My mind raced as I worried how we would set our company apart from the situation at hand. The amount of money owed to us was in the multiple six-figure range; panic had set in. I didn't have any answers, I felt completely hopeless. All of our hopes and dreams were held in the hands of auditors. I prayed they would soon see that our business had no involvement in the fraudulent behavior of our customer.

Our situation was in need of emergent and swift action. To save our business, we needed to cut $250,000 from our budget annually for the next several years. At that time in our business, $250,000 was a third of our revenue. I wasn't sure how we were going to do it, but if we wanted to survive, it was our only option. If there is a will, there is a way, right? I was clinging to hope and willing to roll up my sleeves and get to work. The task was daunting, but

I was not ready to just quit and walk away, not without a one heck of a fight.

The first of many cuts started with owner salaries, and then medical benefits. Next, we put a freeze on purchases and hiring replacement staff. We streamlined processes, and maximized production with fewer resources. We diligently worked with vendors to extend payment terms to ninety days. Thankfully, we had good relationships and past payment history with our vendors, so many of them were happy to extend terms. Of course, no one knew the predicament we were in, and for that, I'm truly grateful. That was at least one embarrassing conversation we didn't have to share and endure. We found creative ways to cut expenses further until we were beyond lean. We straddled the line between our doors remaining open or closed.

Manufacturing is a tough industry with constant ups and downs. As you can see, up to now our journey has not always been easy. Times got tough and we had decisions to make, hard ones. Somehow, through careful planning, serious cutting of expenses, and pure grit, we were able to save over $250,000 in both 2008 and 2009. That was a game changer for our business. I am happy to report that we are still in business and we are once again thriving! This is why you should never quit. Things may look terrible and even hopeless at the moment, but with diligence, endurance, tenacity and focused planning, things can change.

At the beginning of 2017, we started to grow again. We reinvested in our business by adding additional countertop options, added more space, and hired more employees. We were awarded a contract to build countertops for a global home furnishing, ready to assemble retailer, a household name that you all would easily recognize.

Looking back over the last decade, I'm proud to say that we never gave up. You will face hard years; you can take that to the bank. It's what you do in those hard times that will set you apart. I don't care what type of business you have, if you quit, you lose.

Often times along my journey I've been asked how I'm able to run a multi-million-dollar company with my husband. Most people tell me they would 'kill' their spouse. I laugh when they say this. Yes, at times, it's challenging, but one thing that is an absolute is our respect for each other. We respect each other's roles, and we don't micromanage. We make a conscious effort to keep business matters at work and personal issues at home.

I genuinely love being an entrepreneur. I enjoy taking chances and being open to different opportunities. When you are open, that's when opportunity knocks. We were invited to an outdoor concert with several mutual friends. It was then that I met a stay-at-home mom who was very successful in a home based network marketing business. I was intrigued and curious about her business, so I approached her. After all, I already knew how to run a successful multimillion-dollar business, and the opportunity to make new female friends sounded fun to me. Not to mention this was a chance to own my own business free from partners – a business that would truly be mine. A business that I could work at from anywhere. I didn't know much at all about network marketing, but I was open to new possibilities.

Getting started was easy; investing a few hundred dollars into a starter package was a lot less worrisome than the hundreds of thousands of dollars it took to get our traditional business started, so that part was a no-brainer. I was very excited for the opportunity to create a different stream of income for our family. I immediately saw the vision of residual income. As an entrepreneur, I understood that in order to have true financial freedom and financial stability, it's imperative to have multiple streams of income.

I got busy building my new business. I joined a health and wellness company because I have a strong passion for empowering and encouraging others to take control of their health. I love to see others succeed with passion and purpose.

Interestingly, I struggled my first year in the network marketing business. I didn't build it overnight, or anywhere near as quickly as I thought I would. The amount of 'no's' I received was astounding. It was a lot tougher than I had ever dreamed. I started to doubt myself and wondered if I was cut out for this industry. I attended meetings and training sessions. I did everything I was supposed to do, and yet I wasn't experiencing success. I invited others to come to home and hotel meetings to learn about our opportunity, only to find they would call and cancel at the last minute. What in the world was I doing wrong? I found myself exhausted from working our traditional business all day, and felt as if I had nothing more to give. I struggled to find the time and energy to do it all. Leaving my family at night, after being gone all day, was quickly becoming an option I no longer wished to entertain. I felt so inadequate, feelings of failure consumed me. I can't tell you how often I thought of quitting. I'm quite sure it was daily. However, through all the rejection and self-doubt, I could still see the vision and value of the network marketing industry.

Our traditional business was tough, but this was tough in a completely different way. I wanted to find a way to have the freedom that the network marketing industry offers without sacrificing time away from family. That's when I found an online coach and mentor who specializes in attraction marketing and online personal branding. I reached out to her on Facebook. I explained my situation, and she listened. She offered solutions that could work with my busy lifestyle. She spoke to my heart, as she was a former traditional business owner and understood the unique difficulties I faced.

She introduced me to another network marketing opportunity, one that was solely built around a social retail model in the health and wellness industry. This company is one that is truly built from your phone through social media and attraction marketing. There would be no more meetings, no more making lists and calling friends/family, and most importantly to me, no more leaving my family at night. It was a perfect fit for my already busy and overbooked schedule.

It took me a few months to work up the courage to switch. It was hard to leave my former business, which included a family member, my business partner who had become a trusted friend, and all the other wonderful friends I made. As difficult as it was, in the end, I had to do what was best for my family and my life. Most importantly, I had to stay true to me.

There is not a business out there like network marketing. It will make you grow in ways you'll never believe you are capable of, and you'll also be broken in ways you can't imagine. You can't possibly fathom how fragile you can be until you try this business. Yet, in the same breath, you can be lifted so high by the most encouraging leaders, mentors and friends. I'm so glad I had the courage to try a different company. Just because something doesn't work out for you the first time, doesn't mean it won't if you try again. The key is to stay true to yourself, and everything will fall into place. I'm so glad I didn't give up. I'm loving my new health and wellness company and building my business with amazing leaders, mentors and many new friends I've made along the way. I've learned so much from everyone, including my coach and mentor, who has now also become a cherished friend.

I've learned few things along the entrepreneurial road. There will be many ups and downs, don't ride the highs or drown in the lows. Keeping a steady positive mental attitude is key. For me, this does not come easy; I have to invest in myself daily to keep a positive and steady mindset. I take at least thirty minutes a day, every day, to focus on personal development. I love audiobooks and podcasts because it's easy to listen in to the car or while you're out and about.

As an entrepreneur, you have to feed your soul and continue to expand your knowledge in order to avoid hitting your upper limits. No matter what business you are involved with, you have to be willing to grow and change with the times, and be open-minded when new opportunities come along or when change needs to occur. Change is inevitable, in life and in business. Those willing to take action, make sacrifices and embrace change will win.

Invest in yourself. Hire the coach, ask for help and mentoring, take time for personal growth and development, and take chances! It's never easy, but it's always worth it. Never give up! The worst of circumstances can change if you are willing to work hard and fight for your dreams, and don't forget to give yourself a little grace along the way! I'm so glad I said yes. Yes, to taking chances. Yes to the risk(s). Yes to creating a life full of opportunity, dreams, and helping others find their dreams and passions. You never know what life will bring your way, but remember to remain open to all the amazing possibilities!

Lessons Learned and Mindset Tips

Mindset tips:

1. Always stay true to you.

2. No matter what the circumstances are, or how impossible something seems, never ever give up! Remain open to all the possibilities.

3. Remember to give yourself love and grace.

Lessons learned:

1. It's hard to stay true to yourself, it requires you to truly take a look at you, and find out who you really are. Remember to make yourself and your personal development a priority.

2. Sometimes certain circumstances look impossible especially when everything is coming down around you. This is true in both business and in life in general. Never ever give up on your dreams, goals, or anything that is important to you. It's worth it, don't ever give up. In the end, things can and will turn around. Keep an open mind to all the possibilities. There is something amazing waiting for you. This I can attest to.

3. We all make mistakes along the way. No one is perfect. We can all be so hard on ourselves, make sure to remember the one person you need to treat kindly and give grace to, is you!

Aha Moments and Self Reflections

Note your Thoughts

Giselle Morell Marin

Always considered the calm in the midst of a storm, Giselle Marin has become somewhat of an Olivia Pope to those closest to her (minus the White House 'Scandal' and insane Shonda Rhimes plot twists). This knack for fixing problems with smart, inventive ideas led her to founding Dreamality Events, an event-planning company focused on bringing amazing occasions to life!

As a busy mom of four, Giselle knows what it's like to lose yourself in the everyday trenches of motherhood. Through the challenges of raising a family while managing a career, Giselle quickly learned the importance of self-care and support, because only when a mom's cup is full will she be able to pour into her family, dreams, and goals. With a passion for helping women in the same trenches, Giselle founded The Mom-Volution Project - a network of women motivating and supporting each other to 'do motherhood' in a new and empowering way!

Find Giselle online:

Websites: www.DreamalityEvents.com
www.Momvolutionproject.com
www.MeetMeAtHello.com

Chapter 9

There's Purpose in the Journey

By Giselle Morell Marin

Entrepreneurship is in my blood. I come from a family of women who launched their businesses long before being an entrepreneur was the 'thing' to be. In fact, if you ask them, they had a different name for it, for them it was 'the hustle'. From my grandmother who migrated to NYC from the Dominican Republic without knowing a word of English, to open a restaurant, to my aunts who to this day export and sell goods to make a living. I guess you could say that the hustle has always been a part of me. So when I decided to leave a comfortable corporate job to pursue mompreneurship, it wasn't surprising to those closest to me.

I am a firm believer that God has a plan for all of us, and while we sometimes do not understand that plan, every chapter in our lives propels us to the next level. I've always trusted in this belief, and it is what has carried me through all the adversity, heartache, and loss throughout my life. It was no different for my journey to mompreneurship; for me, every chapter, every change, every win and every failure has had a lesson that would evolve me to the next level. Because of this belief, I've always approached any big decision in my life prayerfully with a curiosity of where that particular decision could be leading me. This journey was no different.

In 2012, I was approached by a former colleague to join her on her journey as she launched an exciting new venture. This was no small decision to make! I'd celebrated my fifteenth year at a Fortune 500 company, had recently been promoted, and was well on my way to the next level. My home life was also thriving. I'm married to the most supportive man who was not only a great husband, but also a great dad to our then ten-year-old son and nine-year-old daughter. Life was good! What better way to continue my success than to leave my comfortable six-figure stable career for one filled with uncertainty (and less pay). So with my parachute in arms, I jumped!

Lesson #1 – Never be afraid to take risks. There is never the perfect time to jump in, and you will always find a reason to not do it.

After fifteen years of 'corporate comfort', I was jumping straight into the unknown. Of course, a jump like this doesn't come without a few midnight panic attacks, and a voice screaming, "Are you insane" in your head.

Here I was, unclear of what the future held for me, but with complete confidence that I was walking towards my purpose. I spent the next eighteen months in this venture, working side by side with the founder as we created, developed and nurtured her vision. My time there was full of triumphs, but it was also laced with struggles. I shared in her joy as we landed each new client, and we also shared few glasses of wine when we sulked after a loss. At the time, I did not realize that this was merely a stop in my journey, a sort of 'training center' for my next stage. My time there was invaluable as I discovered some great business lessons that I could never have learned while sitting behind a corporate desk.

During my time there, the business grew, and so did my family! Eleven years after having my second child, we were blessed with a beautiful baby boy who threw our semi-stable world into chaos. We were beyond ecstatic for this new addition, but jumping into the infant raising life after an eleven-year hiatus threw us for a whirlwind. Middle of the night feedings, early wakeups, diaper changes, and running on an infant's schedule felt new to us. It was a bigger change than I had imagined, and it took some time to get used to our new routine. With the arrival of baby M, my priorities and focus had to change. I had to take a hard pause and evaluate what was best for me, for baby M, our family and of course, the start-up I had been working for. After giving it thought, lots of conversations (with myself, with Jeff, and with God), I had a sit down with the company's founder and we both agreed that like all startups, this venture would need more focus than I could currently provide. This was a hard conversation for both of us. I was about to embark on a stay-at-home journey, which believe it or not, scared me more than any other decision I have ever made.

Although we parted ways, the experience and bond we created while building her vision, bonded us as more than just employer/employee. The joys and heartaches of forming a business are only understood by those that have been through it. I am unbelievably grateful for the lessons I learned under her tutelage, but more importantly for the friendship that was born from our time together.

Lesson #2 – Roll with the punches and embrace the unexpected.

I never envisioned myself as a stay-at-home mom. Up until now, I had been working through it all – high school, college, marriage, and kids! Aside from the brief maternity leave periods, I didn't know what it meant to be a 'stay-at-home mom'. However, I welcomed it as a chance to get my bearings and gain clarity on what I wanted to do moving forward. We often don't see what we need in our lives. I began noticing how much my older kids needed me, in the big things, like being at my son's wrestling meets, and bringing my daughter to playdates, to the smaller things, like eating dinner together, and being home when Jeff arrived from a rough day at work and needed someone to vent to. I also bonded with baby M in a way that was completely new to me. It was like being a first-time mom all over again.

I am so grateful for those months at home. My time at home reinforced my 'why', my reason for pressing forward through challenges and working so hard. My family, they are my 'why'. While home, I also took the time to self-evaluate and define my path. I knew that this arrangement was just temporary, a brief opportunity that was a blessing, but I did not want to waste it. I began to think about my goals, my passions, and where I was being led. As I began to self-reflect, there were three things I was sure of:

1. I knew my current work hiatus was only temporary. I give huge kudos to all the moms who dedicate 100% of their time to managing their household. (If you are a stay-at-home mom reading this, you deserve your own holiday! You are stronger than you know and work harder than most of the world gives you credit for.)

2. I wanted to use my strengths and experience to help others in some way, shape or form.

3. I wanted to build something from the ground up. From my previous experience, I saw how much I enjoyed being part of something from its inception and working to make it grow.

I wanted to launch something, but I wasn't clear on what that 'something' was. This wasn't just about launching a business, it was about launching something that I would enjoy building from the ground up. There are two things that I've always had a knack for and enjoyed doing. The first is helping people out, providing guidance, support, clarity around whatever area I could. I've always seen this reflected in my career path and with each job I've held.

The second has been my ability to bring creative ideas and visions to life through various types of events. I absolutely love hearing a concept for an event, and like a puzzle, bringing all the pieces together to create an amazing experience. I love hearing an idea someone may have and being able to bring a full vision out of that idea! Creating events has also always been part of my life in one way or the other. Professionally, all of my past jobs have always had a component of managing and creating events – galas, executive meetings, conferences, etc.

Dreamality Events was launched in 2015 out of my love of helping people bring their visions to life! It was the perfect marriage of event-planning and helping people. I launched my event-planning and design company with a business partner, a year after my working hiatus while four months pregnant with my fourth child. Was I crazy to do this? Absolutely! But when opportunity comes knocking, you don't turn it away, and this was my time.

I had never thought of partnering with someone, but while I was ideating about Dreamality Events, I realized that this venture could be a blessing to someone close to me that had similar interests. I reflected on what a blessing it had been for me to have the opportunity to grow and learn from someone who had launched her vision. I wanted to be a blessing in the same capacity to someone else. Remember when I said that things happen for a reason? I didn't know this at the time, but having a business partner would be instrumental in helping me to get through one of the most difficult trials I would encounter.

Lesson #3 – Find what you are passionate about. Love what you do!

As we launched, we were excited, motivated and ready to conquer the event-planning world. To me, success was a no-brainer. I had the motivation, the background, and the work ethic to make this a success, right? Looking back now, we absolutely did hit the ground running. Jeff was my support system and held family life down while I focused on the business. Shortly after my youngest was born, I took on a part-time job to take some of the financial pressure off our home.

With everything around me running at the speed of light (including myself), it was SO easy to get caught up in the constant hustle and bustle, the running around to try and get everything done. I look back now, and I keep getting a visual of a duck paddling. While he is on the water, you never see him sweat. That was me. My mantra was 'I can do it'. No matter what it was, I felt I could do it. The reality for us moms is that we can't do it all. But here's a secret I'll let you in on...

Lesson #4- NOT BEING ABLE TO DO IT ALL IS OK! Only you can define what YOUR success looks like.

Who told us we needed to be masters of the world and accomplish it all to be successful? I am beyond guilty of taking on more and trying to do more simply because I felt like a failure if I didn't. Are there people that can do more than you can? Absolutely! However, their journey is different from yours and different from mine. Each one has different learnings and different life lessons.

It took a hard hit for me to learn this. I was so caught up in making everything – work, the business, my part-time job, the kids, their school, my home life – that I didn't see the blinking warning lights in front of me with my oldest. Throughout all our changes, our family dynamic had changed. It's easy(er) for adults to roll with the punches, but kids and teens? Not so much.

We had gone from a family of four to a family of six, and as parents, our time was now split in so many different directions. Being pulled in so many different directions, I failed to hear the whispers that something wasn't right with one of my tribe members.

Before I continue, let me give you a brief look at my oldest child. I often say that my first-born is the updated and upgraded male version of me. He is truly an amazing kid, bright and handsome with a great heart that he wears on his sleeve. In his young life, he's been through his share of adversity and pain. He was diagnosed with a form of epidermolysis bullosa (EB) a condition that causes his fragile skin to cut and blister easily. We tried treatment after treatment to find a solution, sometimes only aggravating the problem. Until a community of doctors was able to come together to find an accurate diagnosis, my boy was in insurmountable pain on a constant basis. Seeing your child in constant pain can make you overly protective, with a constant need to create a bubble around them. In many ways, that is what I did. Yes, I know it is impossible to protect your kids from all pain, but by God, I was going to try!

When he was thirteen and I saw signs that were worrisome, the mama bear inside me reared her head. It's hard to pinpoint exactly what I saw in him that worried me. Maybe it was the way he was slowly retreating from us, the dimming of his personality or his newfound attitude that we had never seen. I can only say that it was a mother's intuition. Jeff and I would say things like "it's him being a teenager! He just turned thirteen and is trying to find his place" or "it's a boy thing, they don't like to talk much." However, every time it happened I became queasier and felt that something bigger was occurring. After a while, we noticed signs of self-harm: unusual social media posts, odd text messages to friends, and long sleeve shirts, among other things. After many arguments, discussions, and begging sessions he finally came to us for help. He was hurting emotionally, much more than just the regular sea of hormones and confusion that comes with puberty. At that moment, my world came to a screeching halt. Yes, my clients needed me, the business needed me, but one of my why's needed me the MOST.

Lesson #5 – Always, always remember your WHY.

The mama bear in me took over. Getting him better was our focus above all else. Although my desire was to take a complete pause from my business, I also knew that I would not be helping him by hovering over him 100% of the time, so I did the next best thing. Jeff and I made arrangements in our careers and at home. For Dreamality Events, that meant a slowdown in my focus on the business. This also meant that I would have to relinquish a lot of decisions and tasks to my business partner, which was by no means an easy decision for either of us. At home, it meant that our schedules had to shift a bit. Jeff took on a condensed schedule at work so that our boy would have the support he needed from one of us on a daily basis. We had an amazing network to help us do everything we could to be there for him. From family that watched my little ones while we went to doctor appointments, to friends who prayed for our family and checked in on us to lend an ear when I cried in anger or frustration. They were all there.

Lesson # 6 – Create a strong support network. They are instrumental to your sanity.

An experience like this with your child is life changing. It has a way of bringing everything into perspective and creates clarity on who you are and what truly is important. That's what it did for me. We often profess that everything we do, we do it for our kids. We then use this as a reason to push hard, work harder, and give our all to our careers. I know I did. For years, I worked long hours and made hard sacrifices, all in the name of advancing my career to give my kids a better life. I've missed sports games, school concerts, and class performances for the sake of making a better life for us. I was heading down the same path, only this time with a different culprit – the company I was building. So I made a conscious decision to slow my pace. It wasn't a popular decision, but it was in the best interest of my family and myself. The funny thing is, even though I had to slow the pace, I could still see that there were lessons in this time that I needed to learn before moving along the journey. As I reflect, I now know that part of this was complete divine intervention to continue my evolvement into my purpose.

Through time, patience, prayer, and medical help, we were able to get our son the help he needed. It wasn't easy, and it's still not easy. It's an everyday battle, he has his good days, and not so good days, but I am always grateful that he has another day.

I cannot say that I have reached the end of my journey, or that Dreamality Events won't change throughout this journey. What I can say is that every day is a new lesson, a new experience. With each one, I look to see what I have learned, and how that learning can push me to the next level. Through the heartache and pain, we experienced with our son I met so many other moms in the trenches. Some were trying to master the skill of raising kids without burning out; others tried to manage families without sacrificing careers. This experience created a passion in me for motherhood and for women who dedicate their lives to raising the next generation, but are on the verge of burning out. Out of this experience, I founded Mom-volution, a network of women committed to providing unwavering support and encouragement for moms in the trenches. Every mom needs support and needs to fill her cup because only a mom whose cup is full will be able to pour into her family.

If there is one thing I am certain of, is that my journey hasn't ended. In fact, this is just the beginning! In the meantime, I will continue learning, evolving and enjoying every second of this ride!

Lessons Learned and Mindset Tips

Lessons learned:

1. **Don't be afraid to take risks**. Some of the best opportunities present themselves as risks! Don't miss out because of fear.

2. **Embrace the unexpected.** Sometimes things will not work out the way we expected. That's ok! The unexpected may be guiding you to your next success.

3. **Always remember your 'why'.** Above all else, always remember the reason why you are on this journey. Let that be your guiding principle in everything you do.

Mindset tips:

1. **Create an attitude of gratitude** - It is so easy to look around us and see everything that is going wrong. In my personal life. I've learned that if I consciously shift my focus from what's going wrong to being grateful, I create a shift in my mind that allows me to look past my current situation and see how it could benefit me in the future.

2. **Embrace YOUR Journey** - The comparison monster is real and can easily creep up on us. But here's the deal, no two journeys are the same. It's easy to sit and compare yourself to the entrepreneur who has more time to devote to their business, their journey, their finish line, and who probably has a completely different purpose. Once we learn to embrace our journey, we relieve some of the pressure from ourselves.

3. **Priority #1, YOU**. I cannot emphasize enough the importance of self-care. Whether you are a working mom, a stay-at-home mom, a new mom or a veteran mom, making self-care a priority is essential to your success. Ten minutes or a few hours, we all need some time to unwind and focus on ourselves.

Aha Moments and Self Reflections

Note your Thoughts

_____

_____

_____

_____

_____

_____

_____

_____

_____

_____

_____

_____

_____

_____

_____

_____

_____

_____

_____

_____

Evelyne Nyairo

Evelyne Nyairo is a socially conscious innovator and the driving force behind the luxurious all-natural skincare line, Ellie Bianca.

Ellie Bianca is a passion project inspired by Evelyne's daughter, the company's namesake. A women's empowerment venture designed to "heal not just the skin, but the soul". Ellie Bianca is a beacon of hope and global connection.

Having achieved her Master's degree in Environmental Management, Evelyne provides strategic planning on high-profile projects worldwide and has held many energy sector leadership positions.

Find Evelyne online:

Website: https://store.elliebianca.com

Chapter 10

The Truth about Being Courageous to Create a Legacy

By Evelyne Nyairo

Being a single mom isn't easy. It wasn't easy when I was a university student, working a part-time job to save up for a car and an apartment for my baby girl and me. It wasn't easy when I was working a corporate job downtown while earning my master's degree and doing my best to make it home to tuck my daughter into bed at night. And it's not easy now, running my businesses while raising an amazing, independent fourteen-year-old.

But there's no way I could do it without my daughter, Ellie.

From the beginning, my daughter has been my reason to work hard, not an excuse to put my dreams on hold. Ellie is at the center of it all. What better inspiration could there be in my life than setting an example for my daughter that she can do anything if she works at it?

That wasn't my first thought when I became pregnant with Ellie unexpectedly. I thought my dreams of a life of travel and work were extinguished. I was very young and in a foreign country, it wasn't exactly an obvious jumping off point to motherhood and success. When I held Ellie in my arms for the first time, I felt a shift. It wasn't about reimagining my entire life with some giant, unplanned obstacle in the way. No. My life became about creating a world worthy of my daughter. I was driven to do my absolute best in the situation. It took many hours of study and working multiple jobs, including the early morning paper route I had before going to work downtown. Plus there were the years of accounting for every cent I earned. But through the years, I've built several businesses, and to crown it all, one that bears my daughter's name.

Parenting is tough. Add a business that your little family relies on to put food on the table and the stakes are even higher. When Ellie was younger, before I became an entrepreneur, I was a senior manager in a downtown office setting. Expectations were high, and deadlines were tight. Like millions of women before me, I had to balance motherhood and my career. One of the most important things I did was build a community of support around me to make sure Ellie was in good hands when I couldn't be there. In the early days that meant a nanny, and it's always meant trusted friends who could pick her up from school, or dance or violin lessons. It really takes a village to raise a child, especially if her mother has a dream, too.

I grew up in a big family in Kenya. I'm the youngest of eight, born a while after my other siblings when my mother was forty-eight. That meant I had a lot of sibling babysitters. When I moved to Canada at sixteen to attend university, I needed to build my community from scratch. I know now that without the people who have helped me care for Ellie over the years that I wouldn't be where I am today. In addition to the last-minute pick-ups when meetings run long or clients move up deadlines, I have friends who will have Ellie stay over when I take overseas business trips. My mom will even come from Kenya or my sisters from the United States to take care of her while I'm away building my business. Everyone's community is going to look a little different. The important part is that you surround yourself with people who lift you up. Don't shy away from asking for help. You don't need to do it alone.

Now that I'm running both a consultancy and a luxury skincare brand alongside managing three other businesses, I feel a lot of the same deadline pressure as I did in a corporate setting. This isn't the kind of business that's tailored for working from home in my PJs. It's dealing with government bureaucracy and attending trade shows and delivering on promises on time. I've learned so much that I've become comfortable taking risks in my business. I've gathered enough knowledge that should I need to start again from scratch someday, and I'm ready for that challenge. I know how to write a business plan, and I know that when I follow a good plan, it will be successful. In other words, I can trust the process.

Part of my comfort comes from having a Plan B. For example, my mother convinced me to purchase properties in Kenya, which has become an income stream. It means if I ever want to move back to Africa, I'll have a landing pad and reliable income. Similarly, when the North American energy industry foundered most recently, I moved more of my business overseas. (Importantly, a man is not a Plan B. There are many women who feel stuck in bad relationships or marriages because of their reliance on another person. Create a reliable Plan B.)

Over the years, I've built the essential skills of self-motivation and focus. When I mentor other entrepreneurs, these are recurring struggles. First, there are the distractions. We've got to be extremely organized, especially those of us who are moms running businesses. There needs to be a clear line between moneymaking tasks and administrative tasks – the latter includes cleaning and chores. Your business won't get to the next level if you're sucked into doing dishes all the time. There are going to be some long hours if you want to turn what was once a hobby into a business that pays the bills. For that reason, I advise being intentional about all things business-related. That starts as simply with having an end goal. You don't need to know what the middle looks like, as long as you at least start with a goal that you really care about. Along with that comes establishing a reason for pursuing your business. It needs to be a motivating enough reason that whenever you struggle or get derailed; you can remember that 'why' and get back to it.

My 'why' is my daughter. Perhaps I've added extra pressure on myself by naming my natural skin care business after her. But it's the best kind of pressure. I knew the branding for my business felt right when we developed it to be more than just natural skin care products. It's also about supporting women-run businesses where we source our raw materials and supporting the kind of beauty and strength in other women that I see in my own daughter. Every time I work on my business, I'm doing something to create a better world for Ellie. This connection is essential for me to balance motherhood and business.

Actually, 'balance' may not be the right word. I struggle with 'balance'. I know myself well enough to understand that I am someone who goes all in or doesn't go at all. I'm driven by challenges and results, and I am not afraid to work very hard to achieve success. This doesn't mean I don't have any fun – it just means I have to put those fun things on my to-do list and in my calendar. My daily to-do list has six things on it, and my goal is to get three done. If I get four done, that's a bonus. The list is a mix of work tasks and running, skiing or the gym. Without my workouts, I'd probably go a bit crazy. Today at 6 am, I was calling a client in Cairo while at the gym. It was one thing off my list that I wouldn't have to worry about later in the day. Work is my lifestyle. I thrive when I'm writing text messages on the chairlift or making a call between sets at the gym. The key is that I found what works for me.

Yes, I can be that person who's late for a meeting once in a while because I'm taking care of my daughter. I'm not sorry. I don't feel the least bit guilty. I don't believe we can use our children as an excuse for why we're unsuccessful. (Can you imagine the amount of guilt our kids would feel?) Is it our job is to support them? Yes. But they're their own individual human beings. They're not the reason we shouldn't pursue the life we want. Ellie and I live in a no-guilt zone because I know what's important to me. I make my life and mindset about those things.

Part of my approach is also helping Ellie manage expectations. It's all well and good to say I don't feel guilty about not baking perfect macarons for her school event, but if she feels bad about those kinds of things, we'll both be unhappy. It comes back to authenticity. I believe that being honest about not being able to achieve perfection everywhere is a big part of being happy. Just as we adults know (or try to remind ourselves) that the beautiful photos we see from friends on social media rarely tell the whole story (like the messy kitchen just outside the frame, or the tears that came before the group shot), our kids need to know what's reality and what's the illusion of greener grass.

I know that the mindset shift away from guilt or comparing our lives to someone else can be tough. I was brought up to worry less about what other people think and more about accepting where I'm at and doing my best with it. My dad always told me, "Don't let anybody tell you 'no'. Go figure it out." (Thank you, Dad!) If you find it a struggle to kick the habits of feeling guilty, break it into smaller tasks and just put one of them on your to-do list on any given day. The best way I've found to get through everything on your plate is to cut it into smaller pieces.

I sometimes need more than the (amazing) help my friends provide. I need my daughter to feel comfortable with independence. To do that I've had to let her try to fail at some things in life. Rather than being so close that I catch her before she falls, I let her take those steps alone and I'm nearby to help her figure out a solution when she needs it. When we give our children the room they need to feel out the world, they grow into it. Ellie has grown into a partner alongside me, and she continues to inspire me to pursue my dreams.

The other day when I got home from a long day of work, she'd drawn me a bath. She told me to go relax while she made dinner. (Her signature salmon, vegetables and salad is a favorite of mine.) She's beyond independent. She's thoughtful and resourceful. Recently, we picked out a new bedroom set for her at Ikea. Ellie organized our friend and his truck to help us transport it all. Then, I suggested she make plans to get the same friend to help assemble the furniture.

I woke up at 5 am the morning after we put the new furniture in her room. I followed banging sounds downstairs. "Ellie, what's going on?" I asked.

"I'm not waiting, Mom!" She'd already assembled her desk and her bed. It's just one of the skills she'll already have ready when she eventually starts building her adult life. Ellie has a great habit of always presenting solutions when she's up against a problem. It's never whining or complaining. It's tackling the problem with whatever skills she has. I hope I've modeled that for her over the years. I gave her space to grow, and she gives me the bandwidth to make my business a success.

Of course, it's not just about stepping back and letting your children figure things out. If I went to work every day with my business as my only concern, both Ellie and I would probably end the day dissatisfied or worse. We have two regular things that are key and that we've done since she was little. The first is that we always ask each other about how our days went. I started this when I was in my busy corporate job and had a nanny. I always made the time to ask her about her day. It's simple enough, and this isn't just about going through the motions, but about really talking to one another. It's a chance to open up about victories and struggles, to learn the art of a good conversation, and to unglue ourselves from the screens all around us. Ellie's gotten really good at it, too. It used to be that I would have to coax the daily details out of her. Now, she comes at me with specific questions about sales at work or about feedback on a recent trade show. She's my biggest cheerleader. She is never an excuse, but always a reason for being and doing who I am and what I do.

The second big piece is our regular date nights. I love our date nights. We both look forward to it. It's one of those beloved items on my to-do list. She knows I'm busy and that slowing things down makes us both happier. We take the time to pick a restaurant, dress up nice, and go out. We stick to Ellie's rule, no phones allowed. Then we sit and talk and laugh and she tells me about her day.

Being a single parent is tough. Running a business requires lots of energy. For me, there's no other way I could do what I do it without the inspiration my daughter gives me.

Lessons Learned and Mindset Tips

Lessons learned:

1. Know what motivates you and create conditions so that you can get that motivation.

2. Give your children room to grow into the world and they will give you room to succeed.

3. Allow for dedicated time with your kids. They're as important to your business as you are.

Mindset tips:

1. Your guilt is not doing you any favors. Stop feeling guilty.

2. See your children as motivation for pursuing your dreams, not obstacles.

3. Be intentional in all things related to your business so you can see results.

Aha Moments and Self Reflections

Note your Thoughts

Marcia O'Malley

Marcia O'Malley is a storyteller and founder of Mindful Media Services. She uses video to share stories of amazing people, remarkable businesses, and exceptional organizations. Stories that help make connections, increase awareness and understanding, and ultimately, build a stronger community.

Twenty years ago, Marcia gave birth to a beautiful boy named Ian who has Down syndrome. With the mama bear ferocity of any parent, she's spent a great deal of those twenty years advocating for people with disabilities, to support and share not just Ian's, but everyone's dreams of a bright future. Marcia lives with Rick, her husband of almost thirty years, and Ian on a hilltop overlooking the beautiful Sierra Nevada mountain range.

Find Marcia online:

Website: www.mindfulmediaservices.com
Facebook: www.facebook.com/MindfulMediaServices
LinkedIn: www.linkedin.com/in/mindfulmediaservices
Youtube: www.youtube.com/user/MindfulMediaVideo

Chapter 11

Pulling the Curtains Back

By Marcia O'Malley

I stood there in the baby nursery, barefoot and dressed in my nursing nightgown. I had been moved out of the labor and delivery room and given time to shower and settle into my new room. The baby in the layette looked like a stranger. Certainly not the beautiful pink-cheeked bundle of love that had suckled on my breast a few hours ago. This baby's skin was gray, and he had a dull, passive expression on his tiny face. Surely someone switched babies! I soon learned that he was having difficulty breathing and was in a waiting line to be admitted to the neonatal intensive care unit. A team of resident doctors stood in front of me, and one doctor asked why my first child had died...I don't remember much of anything else he said except that they wanted to test our son for Down syndrome. My ears were ringing. It was as if a semi-truck had run right over me and I was tumbling down a ravine.

After the death of my son Kelsey four years before, I had just wanted to disappear. I had been accused of murdering him. Although the erroneous charges were eventually dropped, the shame and guilt I experienced at that time still sits deep in my heart and follows me like a perpetual mudslide.

I will never forget the day of my arrest. I was escorted to jail by two detectives in the morning and was released on bail in time to be home to watch the first local evening newscast. I was the lead story! They even showed my mug shot. My sister said the picture was so bad that no one would recognize me, and I certainly hoped that was true. I still have the newspaper articles and editorials written about my son's death and me. It was not the way I had envisioned making my mark on this planet.

In the nine months that followed, I heard from friends that people who didn't know me were assuming my guilt before I ever went to trial. I had become water cooler fodder. Anyone who knew me knew the truth of my innocence. This sustained me through the long months of hearings and waiting until the charges were finally dropped. This also supported me as I tried to move on in life after the ordeal. But I still, to this day almost twenty-five years later, fear meeting anyone who lived in my community during that time I worry that I will be recognized as the mother who 'got away with murder'.

At first, I was afraid of all those introductory conversations when people ask, "What do you do? Do you have children? How many?" Over time, I created my own script. I didn't know it at the time, but it was very much like an elevator pitch. I rehearsed it so no matter how uncomfortable the situation, I could easily roll the words off my tongue without hesitation or worry. The story I made up included no mention of any children. I just hoped that if enough time went by, my community would forget. I'd become old news and something else, or someone else would be more compelling.

I took a short break from work after the charges were dropped, but needed a job to help pay our bills. It was the most difficult time of my work life. I started out with a temp agency, had assignments at a handful of local businesses, and occasionally took on contracts for video projects. I stayed hidden for a long time. Then we had Ian.

Today I couldn't be a prouder mother, but when we first had him, I was so scared. I had never been around anyone with Down syndrome, let alone be responsible for caring for a baby with the condition. The fear was all based on the unknown. What did it mean to have Down syndrome? What did we need to do to ensure his health, safety, and well-being? We didn't have a manual with a list of steps to follow. Fortunately, there were many great resources in our community that helped quickly educate us and helped Ian get off to a good start.

When he was about sixteen months old, I enrolled in a nine-month-long leadership development program for parents and young adults with developmental disabilities. This course was life-altering for me. It gave me the tools to become an advocate and taught me how to build community and create change through strong partnerships. These skills have proven invaluable to me in my work as a parent advocate as well as an entrepreneur. Soon after graduating, I had the good fortune of working with the people who ran the program. Together we launched a statewide nonprofit organization to support people with disabilities, and I became its first paid executive director.

One of the first things I did growing up to earn money was babysitting. I had a great gig in high school, caring for children on Sundays during a local Quaker meeting. They affectionately called it Marcia's Meeting. Some of the families hired me during the week too, so it was a great source for referrals. Through this experience, I learned how to organize my busy life. I scheduled my work around school and all my extracurricular activities. As busy as I often was, I was pretty happy with the balance in my life between work, school, family and my social activities. I really loved hanging out with children and being paid to do it. I am the third of five children, so I was used to being around lots of other kids growing up. Babysitting for other people's kids was a natural extension for me. It was also good practice for having my own children later on.

It's so interesting to look back on those days. Little did I know that I was laying a foundation for entrepreneurship and motherhood! I didn't have dreams of building and growing a business of my own. I was just excited to work in the video industry. I had jobs in high-end corporate video production, public access television (remember Wayne's World?), and everything in between…always working for someone else or performing work as an independent contractor. This industry requires creativity and flexibility, two qualities that I thrive on. However, in 2010, I needed to make a big change.

I had been working for the nonprofit organization for almost a decade and was trying to produce video projects on the side. I was doing really important work, helping families across Nevada navigate the complex systems of care for their loved ones with special needs. I helped found the organization and put my heart and soul into my work. However, I was doing too much. The job required a great deal of traveling. In my last year, I think I made six trips to Washington, D.C., and at least four or more to our satellite office in Las Vegas. My husband Rick also traveled a lot, so there were times when one of us would get home in the evening, and the other would leave the next morning.

Believe me, it's not the way to uphold a marriage, and not the best environment to raise a child with special needs. I felt I was failing in every area of my life. Something had to give.

The year before, Rick sustained a life-threatening accident. He had a seizure and blacked out while driving. He flipped his pickup truck and landed upside down, his head only inches away from being crushed by the roof. It turned out that he had an infection in his brain, and had surgery to remove it a day later. He is doing really well now, but the experience left me with a much deeper understanding of the need to appreciate what you have right here, right now; and a lingering fear that something else could happen at any time.

Ian was about to enter middle school. In addition to all the typical fears and anxiety a parent can have at that time, we had the uncertainty of new special education services, at a new school, carried out by new teachers. We didn't know how much support Ian would need at home from us either.

It was during a conversation with a good friend one day that I realized I needed to leave the organization. At that point, I wasn't sure what I really wanted to do, but I knew leaving was imperative for my health and well-being. I was in the midst of menopause and having major issues with the transition. I wasn't taking care of myself, and my body was screaming for attention. I needed more flexibility in my life so I could have more time to take care of my family and myself.

I had always thought about starting my own business, but the timing had never been quite right. I knew at this juncture that if I didn't give it a try, I probably never would. I naïvely thought with all my experience managing a nonprofit and doing freelance and contracted projects, I would know how to run a business. Boy was I wrong! I now compare running a business to having a child.

Even with all the babysitting experience, I had and being part of a large family, nothing prepared me for the harsh reality of caring for a dependent little thing 24/7.

To my credit, when I thought about starting my business I sought out information from our local Small Business Development Center. I knew I needed sound advice from seasoned entrepreneurs if I was going to make this work. I took classes and was mentored. I wrote a business plan of sorts. I never really finished the financials, which in hindsight was a mistake. I learned later how important it is to map out a budget, no matter how rough, so you have something to guide your business. But I moved forward and launched Mindful Media Services in January 2012.

One of the assumptions I had starting out was that I needed a strong brand to grow my business. Get a bold logo, build a rockin' website, and "they will come". Although my initial clients were referrals from people I knew, the business started drying up. I needed to find ways to generate new leads and get more clients.

The other challenge I faced was that I really did not want the public exposure. I was still hiding from my community and still afraid that someone was going to recognize me from Kelsey's death. I truly wanted to be invisible! I also thought my role was to run and manage the business, not be the face of it. I realized quickly that that just wasn't going to work. Today in business people want to know who's behind the name and they really want to get a sense of who you are before they can trust you and actually hire you or buy from you. It's been a process (at times, quite painful), to share my authentic me with the world, but it has been worth every minute!

I'm now very at ease on camera, and I'm pretty comfortable with public speaking. However, I believe there is something about being on video that makes one feel significantly more vulnerable. I think it's because the lens can get very close to your face and peer deeply into your eyes and that scared me. It's as though it sees a piece of your soul. But that is the power of video and why it is so important for people to use it!

I knew that if I didn't come to terms with myself and start using video I wasn't going to be successful. So I have continually challenged myself to use video in every aspect of my business. I also know that because of my experience I'm much better at coaching people to feel safe and confident with video. Yes, it took a lot of learning on my part! The most important thing I discovered was if I wanted to thrive, I would have to pull the curtains back and let the world see me.

One area of business that I've always been challenged by is sales. I don't know if it has anything to do with my years as a Girl Scout when I had to reluctantly sell calendars and cookies (and get bitten by a neighbor's dog in the process!), but I realized a couple of years into my business I needed a mentor who could teach me how to sell. I knew my craft, but I was struggling to close my sales. I found a coach who specializes in direct sales and enrolled in her group program to get started. I now work with her one-on-one, and am sorry I didn't do it sooner! I think it's really important as a business owner to recognize the things that only they can do. Focus on them, and then find people to help you with the other things. It is SO essential to have someone with an objective eye take a look at your business and see where your weak points are and help you build strength in those areas. I've never regretted hiring a coach. She's been well worth the investment.

I changed my work life to accommodate my child's special needs. I'm certainly not unique in this. Most parents of a child with a disability adjust their work life and often quit work to care for their child. I never felt like I compromised. I felt like I was doing the very best that I could for him. To this day, he still thanks me for leaving the nonprofit job and starting my own business. My work has inspired him in many ways. To begin with, he wants to start his own business. He's in his second year of college now and is dreaming about his future. He is very passionate about dancing to Michael Jackson's music, so much so that he wants to become a professional performer. He is my inspiration! When I start doubting my vision, I look at his glowing smile and know that I can do anything! I've never questioned his dreams for himself. He has a natural way of attracting the right people and resources to accomplish anything he sets his mind to. He's a big dreamer and makes a huge impact on everyone he meets.

I'm not sure what the future's going to hold for either of us, but if it's anything like the last few years I know we are both going to make a big mark in the world! The key is to get out of the way, let go of fear and doubt and move forward with great love and big dreams! I may always struggle on some level with being visible, but I find strength with Ian at my side. He's given me purpose and direction that I feared I would never have again.

Lessons Learned and Mindset Tips

Lessons learned:

1. Lose the fear of being visible.

2. Get a business coach to guide you.

3. Stay focused on doing what only you can do, and get help with the rest.

Mindset tips:

1. You can't always control what happens to you, but you can control how you react to it. You always have a choice. Choose positivity!

2. Only surround yourself with people who lift you up.

3. Keep challenging your comfort level. If you are comfortable, you aren't growing!

Aha Moments and Self Reflections

Note your Thoughts

Blanca Pauliukevicius

Blanca Pauliukevicius is a multi-talented entrepreneur as well as an avid traveler. She is educated in finance and has over twenty years of experience in the private and public sector. Blanca has lived and worked in several countries, one of which is the U.K., where she earned her MBA.

She recently founded Eco Art Journeys, a socially minded enterprise that promotes social justice through education, wellness, travel, art and philanthropic collaborations.

Blanca believes in empowerment through our stories, and in impacting the world positively with our talents and resources.

She is a self-taught artist; her recent work can be found on Amazon and on her website. Blanca is a certified psych-intuitive coach and Bravery Architect™ at her own coaching practice, Brave Living Coaching and Latinas Empoderadas. She helps professional women and entrepreneurs realign with their most authentic, joyful lives and businesses. Blanca is originally from Venezuela, of Lithuanian descent and lives in L.A. with her husband and young daughter.

Find Blanca online:

Website: www.blancapauliukevicius.com
Facebook: www.facebook.com/braveryarchitect
Instagram: instagram.com/braveryarchitect

Chapter 12

Healing From the Core to Align with My Soul

By Blanca Pauliukevicius

My motivation, inspiration, and especially my alignment with my job, had dramatically decreased.

I was stuck in a dead-end job, with no support from new management to realign my position and adapt it to what it had become over the years. Even though I felt tempted to look for other jobs, I felt the timing was off because I had a baby a few months prior.

I could not help but feel trapped in a position where I felt undervalued and disconnected. I had been transforming internally, but due to lack of support, my desire for something different made the journey more challenging and stressful. My body was resenting it all...I could feel it.

It didn't help my stress that my little one had stranger anxiety, and we both had a really hard time with separation anxiety. I would hand her over to her teacher, and she would sob and cling to my blouse. As I walked out of the center, I would be in tears too, feeling like the worst mom ever for leaving my daughter like that to go to a place where I was discontent and underappreciated.

I had been exploring the arts for a couple of years at this point. However, I was insecure about my abilities because I had always performed in analytical mode. It was so outside of my comfort zone, expertise, and training. Yet, there I was, sitting at the computer, looking out the window fantasizing about my life outdoors, taking photos or painting, enjoying the sun and connecting with people at a deep level. I was mostly connecting with numbers, charts, and strategic plans.

I had to return to my reality and keep going, because we had lost our home to the real estate recession a few months prior. We were $180,000 in debt, with no assets to show for it. We had decided to move closer to my job in Los Angeles because of my six-hour commute from Corona. That commute nearly ended me, but quitting my job at that time didn't feel like a feasible option.

Losing our home was one of the hardest things we faced as a couple, aside from being unable to conceive. Moving closer to my job would at least make one aspect of our lives more manageable. As hard as it was to leave our home, this move was a blessing in disguise! After years of trying to conceive, miscarriages and being told I could not have babies, within three months of moving I got pregnant with my beautiful miracle child. I was ecstatic because I didn't have to drive; I could actually bike to work! However, things were about to take an interesting turn…

The 'baby-bonding' time had ended when Vicky was five months old. I had to return to work.

This was a confusing time because I dreaded leaving my baby in a stranger's hands. Yet, I was looking forward to the respite of not having to deal with diapers and feedings. The physical and emotional demands of a new baby in my life, along with a foggy memory caused the intense sleep deprivation. This, coupled with an unsupportive work environment, had turned my life into the perfect storm. My life-work balance was far out of reach.

I had struggled with boundaries most of my life, but I wasn't sure why. I would work twelve-hour days, skip lunch to try to keep up with the demands of my job, and attempt to walk or exercise during the day. Stress and meetings seemed to take all my remaining time. This resulted in many visits to my doctors, not only for me but also for my child in her first year in daycare. I ended up with more stress than I could cope with, and my body broke down. Next thing I knew I was placed on medical leave from work because I was losing mobility in my arms.

My identity was crushed because I could no longer 'perform'. I realized something was broken inside, because I knew my identity existed beyond my job. I felt lost, not knowing who I was if I had to choose a different career or job. I fell into depression.

At this point, I was 120 lbs overweight, off work on medical leave with a toddler to care for, and with arms unable to carry a bottle of water. I was in a panic, I felt completely blinded to my purpose and destiny in life. My life felt out of control, and I could only manage very basic tasks

Sometimes when something happens to us, and we are at the hands of loved ones, or anyone older than we are, it marks our self-image and self-belief. Something breaks, and we start believing we are less-than. I felt this happening inside, but I was unable to articulate it, not until I hit rock bottom and I was able to begin my healing journey.

When I began to seek help and guidance from counselors, coaches, and support groups, I became aware of what had been happening. I began to understand why I was unable to have healthy boundaries with work and why I was unable to request help. I noticed how my body felt in the face of confrontation and worked to gain this awareness through mindfulness practices such as Taichi and Qigong.

All my senses awoke, and I felt angry. I had so much that needed to come out, that needed healing. I began by writing and re-writing because our stories do not define us, nor do they determine our destiny. I did not write it from the perspective of a victim anymore, because I am no longer seven years old. I wrote it from the view of the heroine that I am for having endured a lifetime of trauma, trapped in an endless silence.

As I became quiet, more things emerged; hurtful things from my past that I had buried for thirty-five years. I began to realize how I had lost my way to my soul because I was afraid of what I was going to uncover. What happened had hurt my soul deeply. I had been blocking the abuse in my subconscious mind, resulting in my feelings of unworthiness and the need to outperform others so I could feel valuable enough to keep around. As I allowed myself the grace the just be and not do so much, the healing began.

As I re-wrote my story form a heroine's perspective, I slowly began to accept what had happened and started to move on. It was not easy at all! It comes and goes in waves, sometimes things may trigger those memories, but I have the awareness and tools to cope.

After eight months of daily therapies and treatments, I did not see any significant improvement in my physical symptoms. It started to think that I might not be able to do the same work anymore. One of my practitioners told me, "The only way to get rid of this pain is for you to leave your job." I was devastated by this reality. I was comfortable with the lifestyle this career had provided me. However, at the same time, I felt excitement and anticipation set in!

Even though I was in my comfort zone at a job I was good at, I wanted more meaning and more alignment with who I had become. However, I was terrified of leaving a job that gave me satisfaction! Yet, to see I was valuing myself based on my performance rocked me to my core; I did not want that for myself. I wanted to value myself for who I was. I hadn't realized how big of a role my job played in my identity.

But things were looking brighter! I knew where to find myself. I had to heal from my core and change my beliefs about who I am.

Who am I then? I began to ask myself. Why do I love to take pictures and spend hours in the darkroom, or make art for hours and hours? Who is this person?

I had no idea that I had so many passions and talents because I never gave myself permission to explore different things or the opportunity to ask myself what I truly love to do. I began asking those questions. What do I want to do with my life? What brings me joy? What ignites my life and what are my passions, my calling, and my vision?

I began spending time making art and doing things that brought me calm and joy.

I engaged my therapist and coaches. I attended retreats and increased my self-care levels. I began to love myself even when part of me still didn't feel worth loving. I took steps of faith and invested in my healing, in my development, and in what my body told me I needed. I shut down my horrid inner critic and told it to go take a hike.

I began to dismiss those 'should haves' that were ruling my decisions and causing so much pressure. I shifted my perspective of seeing my medical leave as a punishment or something to be embarrassed about, to seeing it as well deserved time off to heal and to realign with my soul.

I bought books on finding your purpose and began journaling like there was no tomorrow. I had so much inside that needed to come out that I filled many journals in a short amount of time. I took numerous classes, retreats, and courses, and did my best to support myself on this healing journey.

It took me several months to start listening to myself, to my body and to my needs…the whole journey has taken almost four years, quite intense but so worth it!

Now, when I catch myself with the desire to constantly be productive or 'make good use' of my time in spite of my exhaustion, I redirect myself to focus on the main priority – leaving time to recharge and practice self-care.

Part of my practice to keep tuning in is Qigong and nature walks. I practice several times a week – this is my self-care. I have created support around it to allow myself to have that time of mindfulness, even if I need to hire a babysitter/driver to take my daughter to daycare.

This work has also been incredibly healing and powerful!

I now incorporate it into my coaching process as part of the tools for helping other women align with their souls. Creating these new neural pathways is not easy, but it can be done. Your body is going to want to keep walking the same route, but you will intentionally take the new route, you will choose new responses and behaviors that support your commitment to growth and healing.

I have to say, this work of healing and growing is frigging hard! Most people avoid it. That is why they won't reach their full potential, because fear paralyzes many people. Facing our fears is the only way through to the other side, to our amazing soul and our passionate purpose. That's where the concept of bravery comes in.

Bravery means feeling the fear and doing it anyway.

So keep showing up, and keep reaching out. Keep doing the things that support your sanity, bring you joy, and feed your soul. Find a good mentor or coach to help you navigate your blind spots. That alone has been an incredibly healing experience that has catapulted me to fiercely pursue my passions and keep listening deeply to my soul. Working with my coaches led me to grow exponentially. Otherwise, it could have taken me years.

If you feel lost in your purpose, and feel like your job is not where you see yourself in the next five to ten years, start asking yourself some of these questions:

If money was not an issue and I could do anything I wanted with my time, what would I do?

What brings me joy? And why?

What do I dislike doing? And why?

What am good at?

What lights my heart on fire?

What breaks my heart?

What does the world need?

What part of my story do I wish was different, and how can I change it for someone else?

How can I create something that includes all the things I love to spend time doing?

What makes me forget to eat?

What would make me get out of bed at 5 am?

What is my vision? What legacy do I want to leave in the world? And how do I merge all I love to fulfill this mission?

I desired travel, to be around nature and art. I wanted to help women heal and align with their souls, so I created a wellness and art retreats company called Eco Art Journeys, and a coaching practice in English and in Spanish called Brave Living Coaching and Latinas Empoderadas.

I tuned in to my core values: authenticity, compassion, determination, courage, justice, integrity, responsibility, respect, kindness, empowerment, freedom, self-care, and passion. These core values and beliefs are the guiding principles for how I want to live. These values inform my thoughts, my actions, and help me determine if I am behaving in alignment with my beliefs and my soul.

Steps of faith, bravery, and determination taught me what I needed to learn to start my own business and to live the life that I desire while helping and empowering other women.

Becoming an entrepreneur is not easy, especially with little ones to care for. The first thing that needs to be in place is an excellent self-care plan because we can easily burn ourselves out as we have to wear so many hats and are very passionate about what we do.

When starting your business you may fall into old patterns of overworking and overwhelm, but you'll then catch yourself and take the new path. You'll have learned what will take you to new heights in your alignment, your calling, and your human experience. Recalibrate and re-focus.

I traded the expectation I had of myself to perform, heal and jump right back to where I left off, for the gratitude of where I stand now. Designing my future, seeing my daughter grow and using all my talents to support and empower women around the world.

Part of the change translated into delegating tasks to others, such as hiring an IT person to help me get my websites and the tech part of my roles under control. Ask for help. Delegate to your partners and children and anyone else around you. Don't take it all upon yourself to do. It's not fair to you or to them.

I also lowered our standards at home so I would not have to feel like things needed to be in a particular order or way. If the house being messy meant I would get some downtime, then it was worth it. I had to learn to be ok with these new standards.

I started cutting myself some slack, and openly acknowledging that I was NOT superwoman. I stood in my power and asked for some of the burdens to be evenly distributed. I also stood up for my needs and goals, such as traveling for training and personal growth. My husband is supportive and has been adjusting to the new me. In fact, he was inspired to leave his job and do what makes him happy! He is now more available to help around the house, and we can even go on dates now. When you transform, others around you have no choice but to grow too.

When we understand our stories and our behaviors, we can turn our lives around.

In two short years, we organized our finances and paid off more than $180,000 of debt from losing our home, making us one of the few debt-free American families.

As I healed, I noticed my emotional eating patterns and began to work with a coach on my mindset and eating behaviors. With the help of bariatric solutions, I have dropped 50 lbs and eliminated the need for my diabetes medication. I can now run after my daughter, and I'm on my way to healing years of bodily abuse.

As I write this, we are selling our possessions to travel the world while our daughter is still little. This detachment from material possessions is also the result of the healing work, because we no longer feel we need material things to prove our worth, or a career to define us or feel respected. I personally believe that our values are what define us.

I redesigned my life now so I can run my coaching and retreat business for women, location-free from my laptop. I do what I love, and I still have time for self-care. I treasure my husband and my daughter, they, along with the women I help to heal from the core to align with their soul, are my priorities.

Lessons Learned and Mindset Tips

Lessons learned:

1. Listen to your heart. If you feel dissatisfied or burned out, ask yourself:

    a. Why is this important?

    b. Why am I striving so hard?

    c. What am I trying to prove?

2. Show yourself more self-respect.

3. Ask yourself, "How I can support myself better to achieve what I want?"

Mindset tips:

1. Ask yourself, "What makes me giddy with excitement and how can I add that to my life?"

2. Invest in yourself. It is important and you are worth it.

3. Set boundaries for yourself to improve mental, physical, and emotional health.

Aha Moments and Self Reflections

Note your Thoughts

_____

_____

_____

_____

_____

_____

_____

_____

_____

_____

_____

_____

_____

_____

_____

_____

_____

_____

_____

_____

Awilda Prignano

Awilda was born and raised in Chicago, IL and currently resides in the NW suburbs. She is the proud mother of a daughter, now grown, whom she raised as a single parent, being widowed very young.

Throughout her life, Awilda has always had two passions – writing and people. These passions are what lead her to be of service to others and pursue coaching as a career. Awilda co-authored the international bestselling book, *Obstacles Equal Opportunities*, published in the spring of 2017.

Awilda is a transformational coach and helps individuals become the best version of themselves through lasting habit change and self-care. She has been through much adversity throughout her life and will admit she is a constant work in progress. Awilda knows first-hand that change is possible when you put your heart and mind into it and remain resilient during challenging times.

Find Awilda online:

Blog: https://laboricuagurl.wordpress.com/
LinkedIn: https://www.linkedin.com/in/awilda-prignano-b5894610/
Instagram: https://www.instagram.com/laboricuagurl/

Chapter 13

The Monkey Grows Wings

By Awilda Prignano

Energy, by definition, is the capacity or power to move and can exist in many forms. I'd been wondering for a while now, where is my energy? For months, I've felt like a little hamster, continuously running on a wheel going nowhere. I woke up every morning with the mindset to do exactly what I should be doing. Going exactly to where I needed to go. Being the person that I should be. Yet, it wasn't feeling right anymore. Something didn't fit. The joy and satisfaction I'd felt being in this place seemed non-existent. The harder I tried, the more things seem to be falling apart. Even before any formal process had begun, I knew that changes were coming. The universe had been sending me signals for a while, but I'd been disregarding the signs. I'd felt the tension in my gut. I couldn't sleep, and I wasn't eating right. I was feeling completely drained. It was strange. Yet somehow, I knew this needed to be part of the journey. This life of constant work that has been a part of me for so long needed to come to an end. My destiny and those I am meant to serve have waited long enough.

Growing up, the world I knew was the world my parents created around us. Their beliefs were our beliefs. They not only had a very strong work ethic but also raised us to believe taking time for family and enjoyment was just as important. My family owned a bodega in Paseo Boricua, a Puerto Rican community in Chicago. Every morning, after helping us prepare for school, my parents would leave together to go to work. When we arrived home from school in the afternoons, my mom would be preparing dinner for us. My dad would arrive much later. We were always so happy to see him and would all run to the door to greet him. As a family, we always looked forward to the weekends. Friday was pizza night. On Saturdays, we would have dinner out as a family. Sunday morning after church, we would have breakfast together at a local diner before my dad would leave to open the bodega, as Sunday was my mom's day off. When my dad arrived later in the day, we would again have dinner out as a family. No matter how busy they were, my parents always made time for us. We got to see shows, take vacations, have picnics and entertain family and friends at home. These are many of my memories of childhood. Not perfect, but I remember we were very happy, and to me, my parents were perfect. Our lives and our home were perfect because this was the world they had created for us. Those beliefs planted into me from a very young age created the image for me of what work should look like.

Once I became a mother myself, my world was different. At twenty-four years old, I was widowed and became a single mother when my daughter was just thirteen months old. As hurt and confused as I was at the time, there was only one thing on my mind: I needed to stay strong to support us. I threw myself into work. I put in the long hours. I took every assignment and did whatever was expected of me. I never made any excuses to not show up or deny an assignment...not even because I was a single mother. I myself hadn't realized this fact until one of my bosses had pointed that out to me. I remember her saying how much she admired how dedicated I was and how she respected the fact I never made excuses for my situation. It made me stop to think. First, how fortunate I was to have the support of so many around me to make this work-life possible: my mom, my mother-in-law, my aunt, my sisters-in-law, friends, co-workers, and anyone that pitched in to help me with my daughter at such a critical time in our lives. I was able to work and provide for us because of the love and support of so many. Second, it made me realize how much of my dad I have in me. My dad worked every single day, no matter what. He never complained. He never made excuses. He always provided for us. Dad was always very generous with his family and friends, but he also made time to enjoy himself. I have so much love and respect for my dad. Hearing this compliment at this moment made me feel a little closer to him.

Eventually, I moved on and went to work at a few other places, always in a management capacity. Leadership was in my blood. I'm just like my dad. Seeing myself in these roles, I always performed the way I would expect my dad would carry himself. Always show up. Be on time. Give your best. Be considerate of others. Be thorough in your work. Stay focused. I did my best to emulate these to make my parents proud.

There was one big difference between their work life and mine. I wasn't feeling any enjoyment. I was so engrossed with my work, but I felt no real joy in what I was doing. There would be plenty of times I would feel satisfaction from a successful executive visit, feedback from customers or being able to host meetings and get compliments from peers. Putting in the long hours and the extra time away from my family was justified by earning bonuses along with other perks and benefits. Feeling satisfaction is not the same as feeling joy. It doesn't feel as fulfilling; it's temporary. The smile is short-lived. My heart still hurts for the moments I've missed being away from my child. All those late nights I got home, and she was already asleep. No matter what company I worked for or capacity I was in, the feelings ended up being the same. It took me a while, but eventually, I came to the realization of how really selfish that kind of environment is. In any corporation, you're working for someone else. It's not about you or your desires, goals, and wants. Sometimes, you're able to mirror what you think your goals are to match theirs. Think about it, what did you have to compromise to get to that conclusion? Is it what you truly desire? Or is it really their goal embedded into you?

Even though I'd come to this realization, I stayed in this environment for many years. Why? Because it was safe. It was always there for me. This was the only way I knew how to do it. I was a single mom with a steady income and regular benefits, working in very reputable companies. Whenever I made a decision to change, there was never a problem getting the next job, usually with more money. With each company I worked at, I was gaining more confidence, and my network was growing. I was feeling pretty good about my status. I was living comfortably. I could afford the things I needed and buy myself the things I wanted. What else is there in life? Why did I still feel empty? Joy. Still no joy. As a matter of fact, when I thought of the word, I didn't feel a connection to it. It almost seemed as if it was a feeling that belonged to someone else. Besides joy, there was something else missing in my life and would take me many years to realize. Something so precious, it is sometimes taken for granted.

Fast forward a few years, and I was finally working at a place where I felt happy. Not every day was perfect, but what is perfect anyway? You roll with the punches and move on. I felt myself in the right place with the right boss and making very good money. I was content. What was the difference? I'm a little older, have experienced a few job losses due to the economy and had to go through the painful process of literally starting over. I was thankful to almost be back financially to where I had left off a few years prior. Reading this last sentence just sounds crazy to me now. I didn't know this then, but I was settling. Settling for what was comfortable and safe. Settling for what I was told I was worth and because I had experienced a loss, I was settling for what I was being offered as enough.

Almost a year into this position, I came across something on my social media page that would make a huge shift in my life, in many ways I would have never imagined. It was an advertisement to become a health coach. I read the ad, scheduled an appointment and met with the clarity coach.

I was hooked. This lifestyle really spoke to me. It touched my heart. I was so drawn. With every conversation I had with the clarity coach, it made more sense. Is this my calling? Is this how I'm meant to serve other people? It was something that until that moment had never crossed my mind. I'd always seen myself as a leader in business because that's how I saw my dad do it and I thought I was destined to do it this way too. After some thought and consideration, I enrolled. I was following my inner voice and intuition. It felt right.

The program as designed was six months long. Each week I was excited to watch the videos and review the lessons. I was very pleased to be getting so much out of this program, both as a student and as a client participating in the weekly skills labs. It was during one of these skills lab exercises that I had a huge 'aha' moment. The other student was probing about what it is that I really wanted. I kept saying things like more rest, more money, and more time. She kept probing, and it finally came out. I was starving for freedom. For most of my adult life, I've felt trapped and confined. I've always had some kind of commitment or obligation. My time has never been my own. This made me think about my work and the feeling of emptiness. Is this where I'm missing my joy? Freedom?

It made me think of my parents, and then I finally made the connection. My parents were entrepreneurs. My dad ran a business, but it was his own, not part of a corporation. My parents worked hard, but their time was their own. Then it came to me. All those little choices on a daily basis my dad made to spend more time with me, was because he could. Every day of my sophomore year until I had my driver's license, my dad drove me to school so we could spend time – just the two of us – talking. When I was learning to drive, we got up extra early so we could have time for me to practice before dropping me off at school. When I was a new driver, I ran out of gas once, and my dad met with me in the middle of the day to help me out and take care of the car. My dad was able to do all these things because he was in control of his own time and because my mom was his partner. They had the freedom to choose how to do things. Being able to layer family time with work is how they were able to find a healthy balance. There were many days that were long and not easy, especially for my dad. But I know my dad loved the community his bodega served, and many of his customers became close friends.

This made me really think about how I was going to move forward once I was done with my certification. When would I be ready to make that jump from corporate job to entrepreneur? I continued the course through to completion thanks to my loyal skills lab partner. We kept each other on track and held each other accountable to finish on time with the rest of the class. A couple months after completion, we finally met at a live event in Las Vegas. Feeling the energy and the vibe of our course leaders and the other health coaches at the event was truly inspiring to me. At this event, a new grad course was presented as the next step into transformational coaching. That little voice inside of me was telling me to do it. My brain was saying no, it was too expensive. I slept on it. The next day, I followed the little voice inside me and signed up for that course. It was a year-long commitment, and the price was double what the original course cost. I was totally following my gut intuition on this one. I had enough for the down payment and decided I would figure out the rest once I got home.

At a special luncheon for the students that had signed up for the grad class, they had a mug for us. The course emblem was on the one side, and the other had the motto, 'Proceed as if success is inevitable'. From that moment on, I decided that was my anthem. I chanted those very words to myself every day. I totally believed in their power. That helped get me through some of the most trying times and some difficult decisions I had to make that year.

After I received my second certification, I again thought about what to do next. When would I be ready to make the move? Could I start to see clients on a part-time basis while running another business full-time? I was drained and exhausted daily from the demands of my position. I had little to no energy to get myself through the day, much less layer in new clients to work with. How was I going to make this transition? It was during this time a new opportunity presented itself- to be a co-author of a compilation book. My time at work was demanding, but I wasn't going to pass up an opportunity like this. It has always been my dream to be published as a writer. The book was published and became an international bestseller. It was in those same moments I suddenly felt a shift in my personal timeline of when certain events would occur, and all would finally fall into place.

It was just one day after the full solar eclipse, and the energy was still full and abundant. I remember there was so much speculation and excitement around this. I found it to be perfect timing to coincide with the major shift I was about to embark on. I wasn't exactly prepared, but when the time finally came, I felt pure joy and freedom. Leaving the building for the last time and walking toward my car, I felt this rush of calm and relief. I felt the pressure leave my back and it was as if I was finally able to spread my wings.

An entrepreneur is finally born. Their influence is always with me. I know they're proud.

Lessons Learned and Mindset Tips

Lessons learned:

1. Staying safe in a corporate position was keeping me small. I was settling for what I thought was enough and was allowing others to determine my worth.

2. Feeling satisfaction is not the same as the fulfilling feeling of pure joy and freedom.

3. Always trust your intuition – that 'gut feeling'. It's always been the push that led me to the change or shift I needed.

Mindset tips:

1. Honor your parents (your roots), their values and work ethic that they instilled into you as a child.

2. Always value yourself and honor your need for self-care. The better you take care of yourself, the better you'll take care of everyone and everything else around you.

3. Don't ever give up on your dreams. You are never too old to make the changes or shifts you need to live your best life. Always leave yourself open to new opportunities. The possibilities are endless.

Aha Moments and Self Reflections

Note your Thoughts

_____

_____

_____

_____

_____

_____

_____

_____

_____

_____

_____

_____

_____

_____

_____

_____

_____

_____

_____

_____

Awilda González Reyes

Awilda González Reyes is a Puerto Rican writer, with a background in mental health and workforce development. She has dedicated her career assisting clients to become self-reliant by defining, pursuing, and achieving their goals.

As a mother and a grandmother, Awilda is familiar with the struggles in parenting, having a career, and maintaining her own identity. She has been published in Gozamos.com and was a featured poet at Proyecto Latina. In 2013, two poems closest to her heart, Allegiance and Endangered Species were published in Rebeldes: A Proyecto Latina Anthology. Awilda was also a content writer for The Body Is Not an Apology from November 2014 to August 2015.

She is currently turning life challenges into triumphs through motivational speaking, delving into her blog Atentamente Awilda, and building a consulting business that moves, touches, and inspires her clients into their best life.

Find Awilda online:
Websites: www.awildagr.com
www.awildagonzalezreyes.wordpress.com
LinkedIn: https://www.linkedin.com/in/awildagonzalez/

Chapter 14

The Second Coming

By Awilda González Reyes

If you had told me ten years ago, that at the age of fifty I would be starting all over again with a new path in life, I would have said, "Have you lost your mind?" At fifty I should be settled in my career, easing my way towards retirement, and thinking about all the traveling I will be doing when I clock out from that nine to five job for the last time.

That certainly is not the case! Here I am at the age of fifty, navigating my way through a new journey I never expected. I never saw the major plot twist that was about to hit me head-on. To embark on this new journey of being a mompreneur I had to face some real hard realizations in my life. That has been the hardest part to navigate amid all the other emotions that I have had to face.

I was raised to believe basic principles. You can be anything you want to be, if, you work hard, you can achieve anything you want to achieve if you work hard. To get ahead in life, you must work hard. My whole life I was taught and led to believe that working hard meant success. The working hard I saw daily is not the working hard that would lead me to someday consider being my own boss, the working hard I saw was hard labor.

My parents were the living example of working hard. Neither of them spoke English or were educated beyond the sixth grade. They migrated in 1965 from Puerto Rico to settle in Chicago, Illinois. They came here with $20 dollars in their pocket and a dream to create a better life than the one they left behind in the mountains of Caguas.

Growing up I heard numerous stories about their own upbringing. My mother, the second oldest of five siblings, came from very humble means. She often mentioned having to work in a tobacco field to bring in some of the income for the family, as well as iron clothes for the more affluent families in the surrounding areas. She spoke about those days with much pride, being the first to buy her own mother her first television. She often cried when she spoke of her childhood being poor, sometimes having to wear shoes that were either too small or not wearing any at all until she had the ability to afford and buy her own. My father, the youngest male out of twelve siblings, had a similar background. My grandfather and great-grandfather were also entrepreneurs, working the land and learning trades such as carpentry, barbery, and harvesting coffee from a small portion of land to provide for the family. During a time in history where it was just not easy for Puerto Rican's migrating to the U.S., they still came seeking the American dream. Believing working hard was the only way to make the American dream a reality, work hard is what they did. Mom and Dad worked all their lives working in manufacturing jobs doing hard labor up until they both retired.

That was the example that I saw every day growing up as a teenager. Success meant working a nine to five job or in this case, a 6am - 3pm job, standing all day with no rest. I'm sure that's not what my parents thought of when they came here to pursue the American dream. However, my parents did not want that same type of life for my brother and I. They instilled in us that school was the answer to avoiding hard labor. Mom and Dad worked to pay tuition at the Catholic school I attended as a young child. Not only did they work their regular manual labor job, but they also volunteered during the little spare time they had to receive a discount for tuition. These are examples of arduous work that I saw; the message to me was clear. I just had to work hard in school and then work hard in my career to be successful, or at least that's what I thought.

In my teenage years, I didn't follow the 'normal' route of school, career, marriage, and then a family. In fact, I have done everything backward; I dropped out of high school, had children, worked and then got married. No matter the order, one thing always remained in the back of my mind: all you must do Awilda is work HARD! I did just that, I worked hard in anything that I set my mind on. Believing that not having an HS diploma or some level of higher education wouldn't get me any further than the optician job that I had at the time, I set out on my educational journey with two kids and received my GED. That was enough for me to get the education fever bug and put myself in college. Ten years later, with a divorce under my belt, various job changes, and an additional two kids bringing the grand total to four, I finally graduated with my Bachelor's Degree in Human Development. I was finally ready to move towards my dream job and in the process; help the world become a better place. I was set!

Landing my first job in social services, I dedicated myself to my work and my family, raising four kids on my own while navigating the everyday responsibilities of single parenthood, but also being a woman with a professional career. I tackled every challenge that came my way personally and professionally because that's what I saw my parents do. Work hard, juggle through responsibilities and be a good person. If something wasn't going right, it was because I was just not working hard enough. That was normal for me, it's what I saw growing up, it's what I saw the other women in my family do, it's what I saw the women in my community do. Sacrificing everything, tucking away their dreams, doing only what is necessary, but nothing more. To be a good mother, to be a good wife, and be a good citizen. This is the whirlwind I found myself in for decades. I worked harder to get that next promotion, to get that higher salary that would lead to a better life for my children and me.

Plot Twist! Here I thought I was doing all the right things, not only for myself but also for my family. After my continued quest to be the best woman I could be professionally, I thought my life was complete when I found myself in a new relationship and saw my now adult children becoming independent. I had also found a new role in my life - being a grandmother. My life was now complete, and I could coast through the remainder of my professional life, planning for my retirement. My partner and I spoke often about our future, dreaming of getting married and someday living in a much warmer environment until we finally decide to retire in our motherland, where my parents were born and raised. We had it all planned out, but sometimes you must adjust your plans just a bit, or life takes you on a whirlwind towards another plot twist you never saw coming.

At the end of 2015, we decided to move to sunny Florida, making one of our goals reality. I had always wanted to live in warmer weather, and I was content. Yet life had another plan for me. Shortly after moving to Florida my mother passed unexpectedly at the beginning of 2016. If that was not enough my partner, who had just become my fiancé, also passed suddenly in February of

2016. It felt like my life had been punched out of my being. There I was in Florida without family near to be able to walk me through the ups and downs of living in a new place and the grieving of two very close loved ones. I often found myself at a loss of what to think or feel.

Through that time there was one thing that remained constant, my job. The job I continued to hold would be my saving grace, because if I worked hard enough, then everything would be fine, wouldn't it? I found myself in a whirlwind; no matter how hard I would work nothing was helping.

I decided to start over again, as I had always done during moments of crisis. I decided to move back home to Illinois and shortly after arriving I had already landed a new job. Everything was perfect again, I was back home in the presence of my friends, family, and children. I was scheduled to start working hard, as I always had. At least that's what I thought, until August 11, 2016. Life would once again unbalance my foundation - my father passed away without warning.

I'm sure you're thinking at this point, what else can go wrong? Believe me, those were my exact sentiments. The life that I had worked so hard to create drastically changed in a matter of months.

Guess what I did after burying my dad in Puerto Rico? A few days later, I started that new job that I had been offered and I buried myself in work. Working hard to move forward is all that I knew, it's all that I was comfortable doing, but being comfortable doesn't bring real change or real healing. Being comfortable will always keep you thinking the same and doing the same things repeatedly. So much had changed, yet I wanted things to remain the same as they had always been. That is until I began to really dig deep into my healing process. When I began to process what my life had been like for most of my adult life and much of my professional life, I asked myself what was I working so hard for? I saw my parents in me, I saw the working hard ethic, but what was I working towards, when what I thought I was striving for was pulled from under me?

That's when I began to unravel everything I had been taught throughout my life. I began to realize that at the age of fifty, I could also be a mompreneur. I had to take a leap of faith and be uncomfortable in the process of trying to map out what being my own boss was going to look like.

In August of 2017, I quit my job with an idea of what I wanted to do, but no concrete plan. I was determined that all the talents that I had acquired and all the roles I held, and all the 'other duties as assigned' that I had performed were valuable enough to create my own consulting business.

I want to share some of the things that I learned in that process and some of the things that I began to do to get myself in the right state of mind.

- Lesson 1: Working hard doesn't mean I have to work eight to twelve hours a day to be successful. I can take all the experiences I have gained in my professional life and be my own boss.

- Lesson 2: Just because my life experiences are different from everyone else's does not mean that mine are any less important or that I don't have the intelligence to use those life experiences to catapult me in another direction both personally and professionally.

- Lesson 3: I don't have to do this alone. I need other woman who've had a similar upbringing to unravel the lessons we have been raised to believe; that success constitutes having a job, having children, and getting married. Life is so much more than that, it can include them, but they are not solely the definition of success.

- Lesson 4: Taking a leap also means having a plan. If you don't have a concrete plan, then you'll be trying to navigate a road with no direction, and you will find yourself meeting another roadblock.

- Lesson 5: Don't listen to the naysayers. The way they view success may not be right for you. Your life and your choices are uniquely your story, surround yourself with people that will be your cheerleaders and guide you to where you want to be, not where people expect you to go.

- Lesson 6: Your children do not stop needing you because they are older and out of your home. They are still trying to navigate the same road you are, and if the captain of the boat is rocky, the whole ship is going to sink. They need you as much as you need them.

- Lesson 7: It's ok to start over again, repeatedly. The key is to take every life hurdle and make it a lesson that will fuel you to move towards your best life ever.

Looking back at my life and the valuable lessons I learned from my parents, there is no doubt they will carry me through. However, I've had to redefine what those principles mean for me and how they will continue to impact my life. I remind myself that my journey is different from my parents, what worked for them doesn't necessarily mean it will work for me. Being unapologetic and honoring my pace in the process is key because every so often I am sure to hear that little voice that will try to tell me that I am not working hard enough or that being my own boss it out of my reach. In changing my paradigm, I am also changing my children and grandchildren. Of course, I want them to work towards their dreams. However, I want them to realize that they don't have to work their entire lives in a traditional job. I want them to work smart, not hard, to enjoy themselves in the process of creating their best lives, however they see fit. I have learned that life is just too short not to pursue your dreams. The universe can throw a major plot twist in your way, but it's up to you to realize that you deserve the very best quality of life possible.

I know that it will take a lot of work to create my momprenuership, and I might even have to rework what that looks like as I continue to seek direction to become my own boss. It might mean that I will have to go back to take courses, spend countless hours doing challenging work or even going back to a traditional nine to five until I make it all work. One thing is for sure is that I know my dream of being my own boss and creating the life that I want for myself will be worth all the time and effort. It's the life that I want for myself as well as the legacy I want to leave to my children and grandchildren, just as my parents left a legacy and important life lesson for me.

Lessons Learned and Mindset Tips

Lessons learned:

1. You are the expert of your story – don't let someone else interpret it based on what they think, so share your truth.

2. Trust your Intuition. If it doesn't feel right then it isn't.

3. Starting over is scary, but liberating.

Mindset tips:

1. Be water. Life is like water, there is a time for waves and there is a time for stillness. You have to be fluid to manage both.

2. Be Vulnerable. You don't always have to be strong; there are moments where you just can't.

3. Be patient with the process – you can't rush healing and everyone's healing isn't the same.

Aha Moments and Self Reflections

Note your Thoughts

_____

_____

_____

_____

_____

_____

_____

_____

_____

_____

_____

_____

_____

_____

_____

_____

_____

_____

_____

Ly Smith

Ly Smith is embarking upon a new chapter in her life after living the dream of a stay-at-home to her now fifteen-year-old daughter. She is chief matchmaking officer of B2B Matched, a subscription service she provides to small business owners who don't have time to network within Reno, NV. She created this venture out of her love for local entrepreneurs and gift for making connections that positively impact the biggest little city. Her mission is to make Reno stronger, one small business at a time, by strengthening the community and churning the local economy. She loves building relationships and brainstorming how to enhance those networks.

A huge dreamer, she aspires to become a motivational speaker to thousands with the intent to help others discover their breakthrough and step out of their comfort zone to their next level!

Find Ly online:

Website: www.b2bmatched.com
Facebook: www.facebook.com/networkingexcellence
LinkedIn: www.linkedin.com/in/ly-smith-6051469/

Chapter 15

Outside My Comfort is My Zone

By Ly Smith

If Plan A doesn't work, go to Plan B. Always have a Plan B. That's what my dad taught me as a teenager.

At the age of fourteen, I was convicted with the goal of someday becoming a stay-at-home mother. I never wanted to pay someone else who would see my child's first steps, hear my child's first words and teach my child bad habits that I could certainly provide for free.

So, I set out my Plan A to discern a college and career plan that would allow me to make an abundant amount of money to have enough excess to set aside by the time I was ready to enter motherhood, and not be a financial burden to my family. Maybe you've heard it before; go to school, get a great job, work hard, and maybe accomplish your dream. My Plan B was simply to marry a very rich man who shared my values.

Several years later, I discovered the world of network marketing. I fell in love with the concept of compounding my time and effort through a team of like-minded go-getters, and the idea of accomplishing my financial goals in two to five years. The bad news was that I had almost no idea what I was doing.

I was so naïve to the process of network marketing, the process that exposes incredible things about oneself. I learned that I was ambitiously lazy, had a huge weakness for following through, and ignorance with prospecting and closing a sale. I discovered some gifts too, like the ability to start a conversation with just about anyone, excellent public speaking skills, engaging eye contact, and putting people at ease. However, those strengths didn't matter when I was letting my fears stop me more times than I could start again.

I had a dream, I knew my 'why', and I knew what I needed to do. Those elements are important when you're striving for immense success. Still, year after year, I let fear have its way with me and keep me from tasting true success. I could engage with strangers about their family, occupation, and recreation, but I was afraid to deliver the message of what I had to offer. I would share a presentation, but was afraid to make the close because I didn't like the idea of rejection. If I made the close, I would fail to do a proper follow-up because I feared what they would think of me. I would make one leap forward and two steps back.

Eventually, I married a wonderful, though not so rich man, who aligned with my values and fulfilled my dreams of being a stay-at-home mom. That dream went above and beyond as I ascertained my daughter's profound giftedness, and I opted to homeschool her to sustain her passion for learning.

Twelve years later, with my daughter in her third year at a school that could challenge her, I could consider the next chapter in my life. I had the time to create a new Plan A with the intention to become financially independent through residual income and purpose in creating win-win collaborations with local businesses and a sports-related social media app.

Once again, I had a goal, and I knew my 'why'. I had grown through reading many personal development books and attending years of self-improvement workshops. I no longer concerned myself with what others thought of me. I was dreaming big. I still had fears of rejection, but now I was armed with a mindset aware that the worst response I could get was a no, and I did not have to take that personally.

I wanted to aim high and attain an account with the president of Reno Aces, a 7,000-seat stadium for AAA baseball and soon for semi-pro soccer. 14,000 plus sports enthusiasts playing on the sports app could mean abundant residual income; a win for the both of us. However, I didn't know him personally, and I didn't know how I would get an introduction. If I got the introduction, how would I set the appointment, do my presentation, and close the sale? Before I could give myself analysis paralysis, I took a breath and spoke my intention to the universe.

"I want to share this really cool app with the president of Reno Aces, and show him how it can be a great opportunity for him and the fans."

Within a week, I was in a coffee shop, explaining to a fellow soccer mom how we could use the app as a fundraiser for our club. During our visit, she excused herself to go to the restroom. I watched her hug a gentleman on her way. When she returned, she leaned toward me while looking at the man's direction, and asked, "Do you know who that is?" I shook my head, and she added, "That is the president of Reno Aces."

I thought, Oh my gosh, the universe is listening and testing me! I have a choice to sit here in my comfort zone with a cup of coffee or I can take action and go introduce myself.

I wrapped up my meeting with my fellow soccer mom, gathered up my things, and walked over to the president of Reno Aces. Though I could tell he was engrossed in conversation, I made a gentle interruption. "Excuse me and please pardon the interruption. My name is Ly Smith, and I work with a sports app that I think would benefit you and the fans. May I have your business card, and I will reach out to you with an appointment to give you more details?"

He smiled as he reached for his card.

Several days later, I met with him at his office. I was grateful to see he was dressed casually because I'm quite certain I would have been a hot mess if he had worn a suit.

He greeted me with a warm smile and a firm handshake, then invited me to take a seat at the conference table. I was visibly shaking as I removed my laptop from my bag and opened it on the table. I took a deep breath, thanked him for his time and let him know I was really nervous about meeting him. He questioned me with a curious, "Why?" I responded, "I'm not gonna lie. It's because of your title."

Inside my head, I knew I was being ridiculous because I knew the truth of the matter was he is just a human being like me, and I shouldn't have let his title rattle me the way I did.

He chuckled and said, "It's ok. Don't be nervous. Just show me what you've got." He put me at ease, so I went into my presentation, which I shared with confidence and great enthusiasm because I was genuinely excited about how the app could enhance the experience for the spectators in the stadium, and the additional revenue it could add to the Reno Aces and the community. I answered his questions and concerns with poise and good posture, and he closed our meeting by telling me he needed to share the information with his marketing team and get back to me. I let him know that that sounded great, and I would follow-up with him within a week. We shook hands, and I exited the room feeling accomplished and empowered. I had taken one of the biggest action steps in my entire life; a huge leap out of my comfort zone.

I realized it didn't matter what his response would be. A yes would be fantastic, but a no was ok too. What mattered was that I completed the action I set out to do, I faced my fear and met with someone beyond my circle of influence. It was an exhilarating experience, and I instantly became addicted to that feeling, so I immediately set more action steps and took them.

What I didn't anticipate was what happened in the follow-up process. I waited several days before sending an email. With no response, I spaced out the next additional days in between emails and voicemail messages. I did not want to be a pest, but I was curious to get his feedback.

The universe was kind to me again, as I noticed the president of Reno Aces once again in the same coffee shop as me. Once again, I approached him with a posture and a warm hello. I gently said, "Hi, it's great to see you again. How are you?" After his reply, I added, "I never heard back from you, and I tried several times via email and voicemail."

"Yeah," he replied slowly, "I just don't think this is something that is going to work out for us."

"I see. That's ok. I understand, and I am ok with taking no for an answer. I just would've appreciated the courtesy and respect of a reply in the first place." With my best smile, I concluded, "You have a really great day." I turned away slowly, and I walked back to my seat, feeling like a diva – unstoppable, and ready to take on the world!

And I've never looked back. I have discovered so much about myself since that moment. I have become fierce – a force to be reckoned, a woman with self-respect, a backbone, resilience and a passion for life beyond anything I've ever known.

A few months later, I was at a vision board workshop perusing magazines for images and words that spoke to my mission as an entrepreneur, my purpose of striving for excellence, my love for traveling and craft coffees, and my passion for making win-win connections. There they were in the middle of an ad for a fitness product. The words that reached the center of my soul and breathed new life into me. They became my mantra and have served me well as I pursued my own start-up venture. In any moment of fear, I have struck the infamous Wonder Woman pose with fists on my hips, posture aligned with feet solidly placed beyond the width of my hips, head held high and proclaimed, "Outside my comfort is my zone!"

I have learned how to acknowledge my gifts, clarify my mission, get on it and stay on it with laser focus. I know that fear is inevitable and that I am capable of pushing through it, crushing it with confidence. I now manifest my desires and affirm the possibilities to grow from ordinary to extraordinary.

Where I once woke up dreading my to-do list for the day, I now wake up with gratitude and energy to take on the day with wonder and excitement. Each day is an adventure.

The best part of this incredible breakthrough journey has been witnessing the impact it has made upon my fifteen-year-old daughter, who conquers her fears and takes on her aspirations with courage. Recently, she decided to audition for a lead part in a community theater play. This was her third audition in three years, and she really wanted the part. She prepared well and gave it her all. She had a fantastic moment with the director and walked away proud of what she delivered. That evening, she shared with me her excitement and anticipation for the callback. She said, "Mom, you know it's all your fault if I get this part."

I said, "My fault? What do you mean?"

"Well, you were the one who taught me to speak up for myself, like asking a server for potstickers when we go out for sushi. You taught me how to make eye contact, smile, and give a firm handshake. You taught me how to speak articulately. You put so much confidence in me, and I just know I'm going to get this part, and it's all your fault!"

Just a few hours later, she got the call confirming she landed the lead part. She screamed with delight, and I beamed with pride.

What more can a mompreneur want than to pass along the practice and mantra of "Outside my comfort is my zone!"

Lessons Learned and Mindset Tips

Lessons learned:

1. Having a plan and knowing your 'why' are essential to beginning any journey. But it's the action, particularly overcoming your fear that moves you along that journey.

2. Stepping just beyond your comfort zone puts you into the area where the magic happens. It happens even with baby steps, it doesn't always require a giant leap of faith.

3. Celebrate your victories, even the smallest actions, even before you get a yes or no!

Mindset Tips:

1. Face everything and rise.

2. Getting a 'no' is not something you have to take personally.

3. Adopt the mantra: outside my comfort is MY zone!

Aha Moments and Self Reflections

Note your Thoughts

C.S. Wadlington

C. S. Wadlington was born and raised in Chicago, IL. She enjoys writing fictional stories that include real situations. She has two published novels, Falling and Masquerade. Outside of being a mom and working a nine to five, she writes motivational pieces and mentors new writers. Most recently, C.S. Wadlington has written two short screenplays. She loves the process of writing and is thrilled to continue coming with exciting stories that are true to life, while uplifting others.

Find C.S. Wadlington online:

Instagram: https://www.instagram.com/authorcswadlington/
Twitter: https://twitter.com/cswadlington1
Facebook: https://www.facebook.com/CSWadlington/

Chapter 16

It's Really Happening

By C.S. Wadlington

I was incredibly excited that my dreams of becoming an author and running a business that supported other authors was falling into place. I had spent countless days and nights writing my first novel. My son was too young to know all that went on behind the scenes when I first started writing, but I knew that I would make him proud and provide a bright future for us one day. My website was up, and the book cover was ready. The book was being edited, and there was great progress being made. The quiet girl, from the west side of Chicago, was close to seeing her book in print. Absolutely nothing could bring me down from the incredible fulfillment I felt. It was many years in the making, and my family and friends anxiously waited for the day to come. All I had to do was get the manuscript back from the editor, make corrections and then prepare for self-publishing.

One morning I had been at my nine to five for about an hour. Suddenly, a phone call I received that morning turned my world into chaos and confusion. My head started hurting, and my pulse raced as I tried to a keep a poker face and remain calm. My calm demeanor didn't last long. Tears escaped my eyes as I explained to my boss that I had to leave for the day. Life was about to become painfully different. My enthusiasm about self-publishing my novel was now on indefinite hold.

The Fire Within

In my lifetime, I've heard countless times that everyone is born with a gift. For some people, they know what the gift is at an early age, and you can't see them doing anything else because they're wonderful at it. I have one friend who was styling hair since elementary school and today she owns a salon. Another friend has always wanted to be registered nurse, and now she's been nursing for over thirty years.

For me, it took well into my adult years to know that writing is what I should have been doing all along. Once I discovered writing and had the yearning inside to do it, there was nothing that was going to stop me.

Daydreaming

Take a visit mentally to your childhood. Was there anything in particular that you were really good at? What kept you up at night? Did you daydream while in school about what you wanted to do when you should have been listening to the teacher? As a child, I was a daydreamer. However, I couldn't comprehend what my daydreams were really about. There was always a common thread, but it took life's experiences to realize what I should have been doing. That common thread was storytelling and writing.

As a young child, I would make up stories and characters in my head until I learned how to write them down on paper. I was in love with writing, but I didn't know it. I thought it was a hobby that I liked; I didn't understand that it ran much deeper. I compare it to being in a relationship; in hindsight, you knew you were in love but didn't have the experience to know what loving that person was about before parting ways.

I pursued a different path by working full-time and taking classes that I wasn't interested in, not realizing what I was walking away from. Being a very shy child, writing was where I took my own personal bow because it allowed me to feel confident. Growing up, I didn't know any writers to mentor or help mold me into a professional writer. I just thought I was weird.

As an adult, my normal life consisted of getting a job and becoming good at it, like many of us do. Going for what you were passionate about wasn't in the equation of being successful. Being a writer was something that seemed unattainable; a dream job that was too far in the stars to achieve. I also heard that there was no money to be made by someone starting out as a writer, so I went with what I thought were secure choices. I began to live the life I thought I was going to make me happy, which was a career in business administration. That wasn't where my heart was. My passion for writing was like smoldering fire. For years, I tucked it away nicely in my mental Rolodex.

Balancing Act

For years, I procrastinated and went back and forth in my mind on whether or not I should write my first book. I was working full-time again, and my hang up was, "how could I work, be a good mother and write a book? Where was I going to get the time?" That's not even mentioning that my parents were getting older and Parkinson's disease was taking a toll on my mother's body, and so my visits to see my parents were more frequent. Again, I put writing to the side, until the dreams started happening.

The dreams were of characters and stories. The next thing I knew, I was having scenes played out in my mind while driving. By this time, I knew I had to start writing, and that was the introduction to me writing my first novel. I managed to work full-time, help my son with homework, and spend time with him. After he went to bed, I'd write. Writing my first book took many years, and eventually, I started taking online classes to learn about the art of storytelling.

I was in the trenches of balancing family, friendships, motherhood and pursuing a dream of being a writer. I was fortunate to have a great support system of family and friends to help me with juggling it all. I fell in love with writing again. It didn't matter if I was working on my novel or getting a critique from a class assignment, I felt happy and emotionally charged. I finally understood the euphoria my mother experienced when she talked about her business. Writing put me in that place. It was years in the making, and I thought I was done when I finally wrote the words 'The End'. Little did I know, I was still in the beginning stages of countless rewrites. I got through the process of completing my novel, but there was much more to do. More rewrites, edits, book cover decisions, and marketing.

As I finished my novel, I was in contact with other people who wanted to be writers. A business was brewing in my mind. My goal was to start a business that would help future writers to complete their first book by providing support and assisting with things such as outlines, reference guides, and brainstorming. I learned that I wanted to be a support system for new writers. I wrote some notes to ensure that I'd go back to it after my first novel was published.

The Phone Call

That phone call I received seven years ago crushed my spirit. It killed my drive to publish my first book and launch my writing business. My mother had been rushed to the hospital and was on life support. The next few days were a blur until she earned her wings to heaven. It was by far the worse day of my life; the pain that pierced deep inside my heart seemed unbearable. My mother was very independent, and she took her business as a financial planner very seriously, because she loved helping people gain more financial freedom.

Within years of her starting her own business, she was diagnosed with Parkinson's disease and diabetes, but she was determined not to allow her illnesses stop her. The Parkinson's disease caused her to be less independent because of the decreased control of her body. However, I watched her continue to work and make any adjustments that were needed for her to get to her office. My dad, my sisters, and I wanted her to slow down, but it wasn't in her to let such a crippling disease physically and mentally stop her.

My mother's death was unexpected. She had been on the phone with a friend talking about financial goals. When my mother became silent, that friend called 911. My mother worked until she took her last breath on her own. When I lost her, writing and starting a business was the last thing on my mind. I wanted to be there for my family. I stopped writing and put my book on hold because a part of me died as well.

Weeks went by, and then a few months. Time was moving quickly and years had gone by while I only wrote at a minimum. Finally, one day I realized that my biggest cheerleader, my mother, would have wanted me to continue pursuing my dreams. It just wasn't in my DNA to give up. I decided to keep at it because I had several reasons that made sense in my mind and heart. She would have wanted me to keep working hard and make it happen. I'm thankful that I found one of my true passions and because of my mom's perseverance over the years, I developed the skills needed.

Motivation

The passion that burns inside of you has to come out so the world can see it. The gift you have is priceless, and nobody can put your unique spin on it but you. Yes, other people can do the same thing as you, but that special stamp that you were born with gives you what you need to make it your own. Have confidence in your pursuit and believe in yourself. As long as the desire is there, you should go for it. At least try, because if you don't, you'll never know the possibilities that can manifest in your life. You don't have to do it all at once. It'll take time. Don't let the process of the ups and downs deter you from starting the dream of owning a business during motherhood. It's your blood, sweat, tears, and sacrifice that will make it all worthwhile. There will be rules. Some you'll have to stick with and with others, you can be bold and do your own thing.

Today I'm still writing and in the process of building my business with new support. It has been a slow process, and there were some setbacks, but I continue to persevere. I've had financial challenges, losses of people I was close to and other things that I decided I needed to re-focus on to get back on the path of being a mompreneur.

Getting organized was a big factor in pulling it together again. I want and need to be successful at doing my own thing because it is in my spirit and the desire in my heart knows it's what I should be doing. Don't allow people to convince you that you can't do it. With hard work, knowledge, faith, tenacity, and desire, you can be well on your way to becoming your best self in the field you want. Dive in until something happens and know that it's in you to be a wonderful mom and business owner.

Lessons Learned

I have learned many lessons during my journey of becoming a mompreneur. No lesson is more valuable than the other, but all have taught me things that will continue to stay with me for a lifetime.

✓ Expect the unexpected.

Expect some curve balls. Some require little adjustments, whereas other things can turn your world upside down. The lesson I've learned is that things are going to happen and you'll make it through. The dream might get delayed, but it doesn't mean it has to end. Life is unpredictable most of the time and if you want to do what you want, adjust accordingly.

✓ The dream might change.

You might have wanted to do that something all of your life, but somewhere along the way, your passion and purpose may change. Take a deep breath and take it all in. Maybe that special gift or passion that burns deep inside and is burning to get out is the cursor or introduction for something more. For me, it became being an author and screenwriter. I've learned to go for it.

✓ Giving up will cross your mind.

A feeling of discouragement or lack of understanding can push your mind in a different direction. A little fear might set in, and you'll ask yourself why you're doing what you're doing. My lesson learned was there are going to be highs and lows, and it's just part of the process. The great opportunity might present itself, and then something might happen to halt the production, and you'll start to question yourself and others. I've learned to push forward and change the plan if needed.

✓ Keep learning.

No matter how much you think you know, always make time to learn. With technology and the way things change, there is always something new to learn or something you can improve on. I've learned in writing and trying to start up a business that there are countless things that you need to know. When the opportunity presents itself, you have to know what you're doing and understand what others are talking about in your field of business. Be prepared.

✓ Support will come eventually.

In the beginning, everyone's excited about what you're doing. The reality is, it's your dream, not their dream. The closest of family members and friends aren't familiar with the sacrifices made or why it's taking years to pull everything together to make it as an entrepreneur. I've learned that it's important to have positive people in your life that are in tune with your goals and to talk with you when you're feeling discouraged by the lack of support. It takes time, and the support will eventually come.

✓ Be patient.

Overnight success does happen, but if you talk to the majority of people who are actively running businesses and are successful, it didn't happen right away. I've learned that patience is needed, especially when you're working with other people. I have entered projects with others in the past that have stalled for various reasons. In the business of writing there are collaborations and solo efforts that run in slow motion at times, but when the opportunities are presented, be ready.

Experience and lessons prepare you for success. Some lessons need to be taken multiple times before you'll comprehend them. The main thing is to learn from the lessons and keep pursuing your dreams.

Lessons Learned and Mindset Tips

Lessons learned:

1. Keep learning because gaining knowledge is ongoing.

2. Be patient. The right time will come.

3. It's all right if the dream takes a turn in a different direction. Change is for our protection.

Mindset tips:

1. Believing anything is possible.

2. Walking in your truth to allow yourself to soar.

3. Have a positive outlook.

Aha Moments and Self Reflections

Note your Thoughts

_____

_____

_____

_____

_____

_____

_____

_____

_____

_____

_____

_____

_____

_____

_____

_____

_____

_____

_____

_____

Shannon Watkins

Shannon is a networking marketing warrior. While raising her four boys single-handedly, she grew her business to be a top income earner to achieve Millionaire Club status within three years of starting her business. She is passionate about helping other women find their confidence and discover their passion in life while learning to DREAM BIGGER with God. Shannon is a single, work at home, homeschooling mom to four amazing boys. She has faced obstacles, trials, and tribulations in the rollercoaster of life. While on the journey has learned to find joy and a hope that the best is still yet to come. There are still many stories yet to come by the greatest author of all time.

Stay tuned, Shannon is just getting started.

Find Shannon online:

Websites: www.GodsWarriorPrincess.com
www.OKCWrapGirl.com
Facebook:www.facebook.com/bikiniready

Chapter 17

Free to Choose Freedom

By Shannon Watkins

I was raising three little boys while my husband worked two jobs. We had one car, zero dollars in the bank, significant debt, and I was desperate for groceries and diapers. But the fact that I only had a GED made finding a job that would make more money than I would spend on daycare very challenging.

Traditional jobs were leaving us just over broke no matter how many extra hours we worked. Babysitting other kids brought in a little extra income, but left me worn out with no quality time for my own children.

A long time ago, I had attended some network marketing training events with my dad, and I was fascinated by stories of successful entrepreneurs living the dream life. Those meetings taught me that there was a different and much better way. Families were making five figures from home or in their RVs or on their houseboats, and never sacrificing their time.

So, when I found myself desperate for income, one particular testimony by a mom raising her babies full-time and still earning a six-figure income kept replaying in my mind. This particular story sent me to the internet to search for network marketing jobs that might help me make an extra $500 a month. I knew working from home would be the best option for my kids and me.

My research landed me on the website of a company that had a great history, mission statement and leadership. I was skeptical about their flagship product, but I knew if it worked, it would make money. As desperate as I was to pull my family out of our debt mess, I would have tried anything. We didn't have the money to spare to invest in the starter kit for the business, but I knew it was what I needed to do. I asked my husband to work a few extra hours to come up with the investment amount, but he refused, stating that it was a scam and there was no way he would let me waste his money.

Months went by, and nothing changed. We still struggled, we still stressed about the bills, we still didn't have enough food on the table. I had had enough. When our tax return came in, I used some of the money from it and invested in our future with my own network marketing business.

I didn't tell my husband because I knew how he would react. I wanted to prove to myself that I could make some money and then I would prove it to him. But, first, I needed to try the product. My dad had always told me that to be successful in sales you needed to sell a product you would share even if you weren't paid for it. That is exactly what I found that day when I tried my first It Works wrap. My stomach had always been the proof of not only the birth of my three children but also my undying love of tacos, and well, honestly, all food. I took my before picture, hoping and praying it would work. The before and after pictures I had seen online boasted amazing results of tightened, toned, and firmer skin in only forty-five minutes.

Knowing that I didn't tell my husband, imagine his surprise as he came home from work for lunch one day and opened the door to find me standing in the living room with my shirt rolled up, and my pants rolled down, attempting to cover myself in cling film to hold the wrap in place while it worked its magic. After his initial shock and trying to figure out exactly what I was doing, his look turned to anger. Actually, anger might have been an understatement. "Please tell me you did not spend my twenty-five dollars on that stupid piece of plastic with goo on it. It's never going to work."

I stood there stunned for a second before finding my words.

"No, I didn't. I bought the $200 starter kit..." my words trailed off as he turned, slammed the door behind him and returned to work without his lunch.

The next forty-five minutes was spent praying this thing would work, that I had not wasted money on a "stupid piece of plastic with goo on it" that wouldn't actually help my mom belly. Thankfully, the wrap did work. When I removed it from my stomach, just forty-five minutes later, my stretch marks went from their regular deep, dark purple (something that resembled surviving a tiger attack) to almost invisible. My stomach just looked better, and I definitely felt better.

I was so excited about my results and so passionate about what I had just found because I knew it would help a lot more people. My desire to tell everyone about what I found overshadowed my usual shyness. I immediately texted the only three people I knew in the city where we had just moved saying, 'Every Mommy needs to message me right now. What I just found is going to change your life...and your tummy'.

When my husband came home from work that night, I was waiting by the front door with my shirt tied up so he could see my new and improved tummy. He was not nearly as excited as I was, and just nodded when I asked if he could see a difference. He then just said, "That's great. Now make me my money back."

For the first time in years, I felt empowered and said, "I already did." That moment forever changed my mindset. I didn't want to ask him for money for diapers for my babies. I didn't want to ask him if I could borrow the car to see a friend. I wanted my own money. I never wanted to depend on anyone ever again. I wanted to make sure my kids never had to go without again. His hateful stare forever etched into my memory as he said, "this won't last," was a driving force in my career for years to come. His doubt in the product, the business, and me, made me set out to prove it all. What would have been a deterrent for most novice network marketers, spurred me on.

The first time I hosted a party, no one showed up. I was devastated, but I didn't let it stop me. I spent the time that was allotted for the party texting others and asking them to have a party for me. My first actual party, twenty-four people rsvp'd. I had never spoken in a room of that many people before. I was so quiet and shy that I suffered through speaking to a group of two or more. I was so nervous that I pulled over twice on the way to the party to throw up. When I got there, my hostess gave me some gum and offered me some reassurance. Since she was a good friend, she stood beside me as I wrapped all the guests and answered their questions about the product with an, "I don't know, but I'll find out."

Each time I stepped out of my comfort zone, I became a little braver. As I did things over and over again, I realized I was good at it, and there was nothing to fear. Before long, I looked back and wondered why I ever thought my comfort zone was 'comfortable', as it now looked like a box confining a terrified, insecure girl.

I dug into the company's online training and became a student of the business and the industry. The more I plugged in, the more my confidence grew in the products. The more my confidence grew in the products, the more people I wanted to tell about them. The more people I told about them, the more sales I made. The more sales I made, the more my paycheck grew. The more my paycheck grew, the more my confidence in the business grew. The more my confidence in the business grew, the more my team grew.

People making fun of my product did not hinder me because I knew it was their loss. I saw my own results, and I saw it work on so many others that nothing would change my mind or my passion for my product.

People making fun of the industry did not slow me down because my business consistently paid my bills. I developed my own strong foundation of belief.

I climbed the ranks quickly in the company, working almost entirely on social media. I was intentional about creating relationships. I watched for needs within my friendships and then shared a solution in the form of a product or opportunity. I asked my friends to host parties for me so I could get in front of their friends. I sought every opportunity to meet new people through classes, mommy playgroups, or even common interest groups on social media. I was always so shy and terrified before parties and events. I had so little self-confidence stemming from years of emotional abuse that it took everything in me to find my twenty seconds of insane courage to do what needed to be done. But I knew I had to do it. My kids deserved it.

I watched top leaders in the company and listened to their training. One thing they all seemed to say was to focus on personal development, as your check can never go higher than your mindset. So I read books on success, books on developing confidence, creating relationships, and books on the network marketing industry itself. I stayed consistent with the things that were working, and I tried new things to continually expand my outreach. Every day I worked my business like a business, and every month it paid like a business.

One payday, my husband was standing behind me as I was checking my commissions online. My jaw dropped when I saw that I had made my first five-figure monthly check less than a year into the business. I turned to look at him to see if he had seen the amount and I knew he had by his widened eyes that were staring at the screen in disbelief.

"Oh my goodness! Do you see this? Look what I did!" I exclaimed.

To which he replied, "Don't get too excited. You did it once, but it won't last."

Not only had it lasted; it had also grown exponentially. I was making more money than I had ever thought possible, and we were living the dream life. We were able to adopt our fourth son, travel whenever and wherever we wanted. We never said no to an opportunity. But keeping up with family life was becoming a struggle. I was juggling the kids, cooking, cleaning, laundry, and a six-figure a year business. My husband left his career in the military and came home to help me with the business and the kids full-time. I knew how much more money we could make with the both of us helping as a power team. Except, he didn't have the passion for the products, the business or the industry. He only had a passion for spending the money he once said I would never make.

And then one day, my entire world shattered. My husband took his 'share' of the business and left my children and me for a new life.

Everything changed overnight.

I began to doubt myself.

Why was I not good enough?

For about six months, I couldn't even think about posting on social media or having a wrap party in my home, and I definitely didn't feel like I could encourage my team or inspire anyone to join me. Some days it was a struggle just to get out of bed or do the everyday mom duties.

However, despite my lack of enthusiasm for work, my business continued to pay well, and I was thankful every single day that God had given me something to provide for my family during this time. I had a nice residual income that allowed me to focus on my children and my healing for as long as I needed to, without worrying about going to work. Work I had done years before was still paying my bills at a time I needed it the most. Had I had a traditional job, I would never have survived long workdays during this time of grief.

However, I didn't want to just survive on what had already been made. I wanted to grow my income again. I knew that I was going to have to find that belief again. The belief in myself that had been stolen. Perhaps some of the greatest advice I've ever been given came to me during this time. It applies to every area of our lives, from marriage, workouts, dieting, and especially our businesses.

Action creates passion. My upline told me, "Don't feel like working? Do it anyway."

And so, I got started again. I watched all of the training videos eight years into the business as if I was a new distributor. I listened to all the calls from successful people. I started hosting parties again. I used my own products consistently. I started posting on social media again. I started talking to people again. Again, my upline's advice rang true. 'Passion is contagious. If you're passionate about your life, your business, and your products, you will attract the right people. We create our own momentum.'

I've definitely learned that to be successful in the direct sales or network marketing industry you need to believe in your products. As my dad said, "Sell something you'd share even if you didn't get paid for it." I absolutely love my products and never want to live without them. If you're looking for extra income from home and considering sales, ask yourself what you are already passionate about. If you couldn't care less about makeup and never wear it, a makeup business probably isn't going to be your launching pad to success. You should definitely be your best customer.

Any successful person in network marketing or direct sales would tell you that it all comes down to belief in three core areas. Belief in yourself is perhaps the most important. When I started in the industry, I didn't have belief in myself. I wasn't happy where I was in life and believed there was something better. I was willing to learn and develop that belief in myself. I was willing to step out of my comfort zone and do whatever it took. When I didn't believe in myself and was surrounded by people who didn't believe in me, I found different people who would believe in me and who had a stronger belief in the industry, products, and business. I would borrow their belief until I developed my own. I learned to quote scriptural affirmations and even write encouraging words to myself on my mirror until I began to believe the things I was saying.

I used my own products and developed my own story and an unshakable belief in what I was selling. I knew what it did for me and what it could do for others. This belief created a contagious passion for my products. What I didn't know, I learned. I listened to others who knew more than myself and again borrowed their knowledge and beliefs when necessary.

My passion and belief in the industry was laid in my mind as a child hearing success stories and knowing that there was a better, yet different path than the traditional job. However, my true passion came from learning my true 'why' of doing the business. I always thought it was to make extra money to provide for my kids, but after the divorce and becoming a single mom of four boys overnight, I now know that it's about freedom. Freedom to grieve, freedom to heal, freedom to be present, freedom to work from home, freedom to take time off and still get paid. Freedom to never depend on anyone else to provide for my children.

Lessons Learned and Mindset Tips

Lessons learned:

1. Work your business like a business and it will pay like a business.

2. Trust the process and be coachable.

3. We create our own momentum.

Mindset tips:

1. You are believe what you are. Not what others say you are.

2. Action creates passion.

3. Failing is not failure- it is about what we need to learn.

Aha Moments and Self Reflections

Note your Thoughts

_____

_____

_____

_____

_____

_____

_____

_____

_____

_____

_____

_____

_____

_____

_____

_____

_____

_____

Carine Werner

Carine's journey is one filled with triumph, passion, determination, and perseverance. Through her vibrant personality and commitment to success, you can learn how to generate success in your business and life.

Early in her career, Carine was self-taught and used her resourcefulness to grow massive success in her business. She realized that being an entrepreneur was her passion and her talent. She leveraged her knowledge to grow a six-figure income from nothing. She now teaches others to leave the grind behind to create time and financial freedom so they can live a fulfilled life.

Carine believes the key to momboss success is leveraging override, recurring, and residual income. She teaches mindset strategies and actionable tools to help make this a reality for her clients Carine is speaker who changes lives, a mentor, and Reiki master.

She lives in Arizona with her husband Matt and their three children.

Find Carine online:

Website: www.askcarine.com
Facebook: www.facebook.com/askcarine
Instagram: www.instagram.com/askcarine

Chapter 18

Trifecta to Success

By Carine Werner

When I began my adventure in entrepreneurship, I was a mom to my beautiful daughter and a wife, so a flexible business was the only option for me. Making the $10-$15 an hour that most companies were offering was simply not enough for me to cover our bills and help my family live the lifestyle we desired. My back was against the wall and I had to make something happen. As moms, we always want the best for our families and our children, and sometimes having a 'j-o-b' is not the ticket for that. I realized that early on that if I wanted to contribute and provide the type of life my family and I dreamed of, I would need to generate the income that I wanted and felt worthy of.

Prior to embarking on this journey, I had devoured personal development books and courses, and people always came to me for advice. I think it was a combination of these two things that really helped me when I decided to dive into the mortgage industry with zero knowledge or experience. I literally knew nothing when I invited myself in for an interview, impressed the manager, and was hired. In the mortgage industry, you have to produce results in order to be paid.

With no real idea of what I needed to do, I started with what I thought would be best. I ordered business cards and started pounding the pavement, driving up and down a major boulevard in my hometown dropping off donuts and business cards to real estate offices. I wanted to get my name out there and turn this opportunity into something wildly successful. That was my game plan. Back then, there was no social media, and I had no marketing budget to speak of.

I remember one time I was in a real estate office passing out business cards and introducing myself to agents when all of a sudden, the managing broker came in and kicked me out because they already had a preferred lender. I left, slightly humiliated, but with a smile. The experience was embarrassing. However, I didn't let it shape me, because I had already made a commitment to myself and to my family that I wanted to create an awesome life for us. I was willing to face anything, even that embarrassment, to make sure that I made good on that commitment.

I did everything I could to make the most of my career. I talked to everyone I knew, and I let them know what I was doing. I also figured out that knowing and marketing the greatest, juiciest loan program available generated interest that I would use to get in front of them.

When I went to take my first loan application, I didn't know anything about mortgages and had no experience. I asked a loan officer about what I needed to collect from the prospect. I handed him a yellow notepad to write everything down. He gave me what I needed, and off I went. I filled in the blanks of the application for the prospect over the course of our meeting. Back then, good-faith estimates and disclosures were hand-written.

Since I didn't know how to calculate some of these things, I told them I would be back to finish up. I collected what I needed and off I went. Back at my office, I grabbed a mortgage account executive and asked for help putting it all together. Some time and an emotional rollercoaster ride later, I closed the loan.

Over the course of working with this brokerage, I discovered that I was not in alignment with that organization, so I went to another mortgage company, a bank this time. It was a boring, treacherous, dry, and stuffy environment. I hated it! However, I was on a mission. While I was there, I invested in a wrap for my car with my advertisement: a picture of me, and information to contact me. Through my 'marketing on wheels', I was recruited to another company. This would be my third since the dawn of my career. This was where things really took a massive turn for me.

Shortly after I was recruited to the new company, I became pregnant with my second child. It was a very complicated pregnancy; I was burdened with headaches and major discomforts. During this time, the CEO of the organization saw something in me that I didn't see in myself at the time.

One night, while I was extremely pregnant with swollen feet and a big plump belly, I was relaxing on the couch, and the phone rang. On the other end was the CEO of the company. He said, "Carine, I think that you're doing really great and you have all of the characteristics I'm looking for. I want you to become a production manager for our company. This means that you will be recruiting, hiring, training, and developing new loan officers." I was shocked! Thoughts were flying through my head. I had never done anything like this before, so how would I make it work? I knew that God looks out for us, so out of my mouth came, "Sure, I'd love to!" I was invited to my first managerial meeting the following week.

After my son was born, I brought him to the office and to manager's meetings. At first, it was a struggle as this was all new to me and my confidence wasn't the greatest, but I kept moving forward, post-pregnancy brain fog and all. At some point, it became apparent to me that the CEO had changed the format of the meetings; we started reading books and discussing our takeaways. Instead of managing us, he began mentoring us. It was through this change in his styles that inspired me to do the same.

Prior this change, I recruited loan officers through newspaper ads, word of mouth, and any other way I could. I was incredibly resourceful, so I made it up as I went along. Between managing and training, I found the work tedious and boring. As a matter of fact, I hated it. To top it off, we weren't producing any results. That is when I flipped the switch. I took my newfound inspiration from the CEO, hired an assistant, and changed my ways. With my new assistant, I was able to leverage her skillset to do things that I did not enjoy, like paperwork, follow-ups, and processing. This was one of the greatest gifts I could have given myself. With my time freed up, I started mentoring and leading the loan officers through coaching and by example. I taught mindset strategies, courage-building techniques, and how to achieve results-driven appointments. I would attend their appointments and help to close the deals. I often closed them myself, but I made it appear as though the loan officer accomplished it. I always empowered and edified each loan officer, which allowed their confidence to grow, lending them my best skills in creating long-lasting referral relationships to help them produce a steady stream of business. It's more effective to show up with confidence than it is to know all of the X's and O's.

Switching from training to coaching and mentoring made a world of difference. Suddenly, our results were astonishing. One loan officer that stands out to me was a young man who came in for an interview. I was not there because my son had had an explosive poop all over his crib. During the clean-up, my office called to let me know I had someone waiting for me. Fortunately, this gentleman gracefully rescheduled for the following day as I was up to my elbows in baby poop! He returned to the office the next day, and I hired him. At the time, he was working for his father's landscape company, making roughly $1500 a month. Within two years, he was earning more than $200,000 per year applying the tools and strategies I taught.

As I rose up in the company and our results increased significantly, I began earning awards and trips. They were the first awards I had ever received in my life. It felt crazy, but good!

To stay focused and goal-oriented I used two mindset tools on a daily basis. They consisted of morning and nighttime rituals that allowed me to stay focused and become clear on what I wanted and needed to do.

Each morning I would visualize the result I wanted to create and then I would set the intention of achieving just that. In lending, not everything is easy. I put myself in each of my client's shoes and asked, "If this were me, would this loan be beneficial for my situation?" This was my starting point for each transaction. There were times when I made things happen that seemed impossible, and I credit this to my confidence and sheer commitment to doing the right thing and taking care of my clients and team.

Each night I would replay my day and review what I could have done better, regardless of whether the day was good or bad. I always wanted to know where I could have done better, and how I could be my best self and produce the best results. Through this, I was teaching and growing myself to be better in all areas of my life.

When it comes to being self-employed and making things work, there are a few tools that you really need to know that will help you generate success. The first tool is a visualization, which I relate to real estate. Imagine that your mind is an apartment complex that you need to fill with tenants. The tenants, however, are 'thoughts' of what you want to create in your life and mindset tools you will use to get there. Always take note of who and what is occupying space in your brain. If you want to create a new result, you need to evict the tenants that are not helping you and replace them with ones that will.

When you want to see results, you need to create a new vision and align yourself with it. I wholly believe in this and used it to create my Trifecta to Success: thoughts, words, and actions (TWA). Everything begins with a thought, so create a vision of your desired result. They are often things you 'think' about as you put your head on your pillow at night, but push away by midday. Align your thoughts with words that support your vision and take action each day, even if it seems small. Be open to and prepared for serendipitous moments and miracles to fall into place

After nearly a decade, I realized that my life no longer had balance or rhythm in it. What started out as my ticket to free time and financial freedom became my biggest burden. After giving birth to my third child, another little boy, I only took a week off for maternity. I had even been working on my phone while in labor. That was not self-care! I knew I wanted something different for my family and myself.

Eventually eliminating the mortgage part of the equation, I dove into personal development and achieved coaching certifications in neurolinguistics, hypnosis, business, life, and success.

During this new and trying journey, I used my Trifecta to Success formula and helped other people produce massive results in their lives. I soon realized that trading time for money and creating and launching new programs was ineffective in creating the wealth and success I wanted for my family.

I wanted a business model that I could work on from anywhere, like my home or vacations. A business that I did not have to rebuild each month. It became clear to me that residual, leveraged and override income are key to creating that. After a few years of research, trial and error, I have achieved the perfect formula.

And that is how I arrived at where I am now!

Now I lead people to success and teach them how they can create time and financial freedom by earning a six-figure income. This includes residual and linear income streams. Both are imperative if you are going to generate the freedom you desire in your life.

I want to leave you with these three lessons to help you realize, visualize, and attract the success you desire into your life:

1. Pick the right vehicle. It is important that you pick an industry where you can set yourself up to either have residual income and/or leverage other people's skills, efforts, and time. Doing this allows you to have the freedom to enjoy the life you are creating, and not feel completely consumed by your business. That complete consumption creates burnout, which can lead to chaos and unhappiness, not only in your business but in your personal life as well. Leveraging residual income, recurring and override income, and aligning yourself with people on the same path gives you the opportunity to live the life you desired to create when you set out on this journey.

2. Have a mentor. When I realized that the CEO of the mortgage company stopped being a manager and started being a

mentor, everything changed for me. When I started mentoring my team rather than managing them, everything changed for them as well. Having a mentor can completely change your experience and chance of success. Find someone who has walked the path before you. Someone who has the tools, skillset and the ability to make things happen for you. Good mentorship is absolutely imperative to creating success. Entrepreneurship can be a lonely place, so you will want to have someone who encourages you, cheers you on, and holds your feet to the fire when necessary. As a result of having strong mentors in my own life, I have become the go-to mentor for many entrepreneurs, because I have the ability to light them up. I believe in them, encourage them, and hold them accountable to get to where they want to go.

3. Never give up – you have to be persistent! Stay committed to your goals, be willing to ignore what you look like or what others think of you, and never stop in the face of anything. If you want something, you can have it. Keep working toward it, learning everything you can, and put the Trifecta to Success to use. Think it. Speak it. Do it.

Lessons Learned and Mindset Tips

Lessons Learned:

1. Trust your intuition and always be open to miracles and serendipitous moments.

2. Walk by faith, you don't have to see or know the path, just be clear of the result you want to achieve and stay in action.

3. Use obstacles as fuel for your journey, that includes naysayers and people who tell you no!

Mindset tips:

1. Everything begins with a thought, so choose your thoughts wisely.

2. Your mind doesn't know the difference between what is real and what is visualized, so focus on what you want, even if it seems impossible.

3. Your subconscious mind is there to make your conscious mind right. It will seek out a match for your most dominant thoughts and give it to you, so actively visualize your vision and desired results daily!

Aha Moments and Self Reflections

Note your Thoughts

Dana Zarcone

Known as 'The Liberating Leadership Coach,' Dana is passionate about helping her clients live all-in and full-out, step into their power, and enjoy epic success in life and business. Following a successful twenty-four-year corporate career, Dana earned her Master's Degree in Counseling.

She works as a national certified counselor, certified Core Energetics practitioner, certified kinesiologist, and leadership coach. Dana provides leadership training as well as individual and group coaching. She's a coach, trainer, motivational speaker, international bestselling author and publisher, and host of The Your Shift Matters podcast.

Dana integrates neuroscience, quantum physics, kinesiology, and psychology to show her clients what is truly possible. Through her broad range of research, working with clients, extensive education and everyday application, Dana has developed a novel approach that has helped hundreds of people make measurable shifts in their lives. Through her revolutionary process, they cultivate positive, long-lasting changes that enable them to reach their fullest potential in mind, body, and spirit.

Find Dana online:
Websites: www.DanaZarcone.com
www.YourShiftMatters.com
Twitter: www.Twitter.com/DanaZarcone

Chapter 19

Mompreneur Madness or Business Bad-Assness?

By Dana Zarcone

I was so excited when I got the call. They told me that they were really impressed with me and that they were offering me a job. They were starting me out with a salary well beyond what I had hoped for and, of course, I said "yes".

I spent the next twenty-four years climbing the proverbial corporate ladder, and I was climbing fast. I was being promoted and relocated every couple of years. Every assignment I had was significantly different from the last. I really appreciated the variety, as I tend to get bored rather quickly.

I was at a high point in my career when I became pregnant with my first daughter, Sierra. I was fortunate. The pregnancy was easy-peasy. In fact, I really enjoyed being pregnant. Then, of course, many months later my whole world was turned upside down, as I was a new mother and had no clue what I was doing!

Being in the U.S., maternity leave came and went in what felt like a blink of an eye. Even though it was short, I had plenty of time to bond with her and really embrace the new, crazy life of being a mother. WOW, I'm a mother! It was surreal, that's for sure.

Reluctantly, I returned to work and was in the throes of juggling a high-profile career while caring for a new born! I quickly learned it's not as easy as other mothers make it look.

I have never felt as guilty as the first day I had to drop her off at daycare. Needless to say, I bawled my eyes out. I didn't want to leave her, especially in the care of someone else. I had a hundred thoughts racing through my mind. *What if she cries and they don't get to her soon enough? What if they accidently give her the wrong milk? What if someone abuses her in some way? Oh Dear Lord. What was I doing leaving her with someone else? How selfish of me!*

The first couple of weeks were the hardest. Then, I started to get back into a rhythm at work and realized how much I enjoyed my career. I began to realize that without feeding the career-oriented, ambitious side of me, I'd be resentful. Being satisfied with what I was doing outside of motherhood is what allowed me to be a really good mother. I know that sounds strange, but it's true.

When you have that burning desire to achieve some pretty lofty goals, it'd be a tragedy to decide not to pursue them. I came to realize that we can have it all, with a little planning and focus! Not to say it's easy…but it's definitely possible and attainable.

Shortly after Sierra was born, we were relocated to Ohio, and I was fortunate to keep my job and work from home. I had a global management job with a lot of responsibility, so the company made me promise that I'd find alternative care for Sierra during work hours. As hard as it was, I knew it was the right thing to do so that

I could give my job the respect, effort, and attention it deserved. After all, I was still climbing that proverbial corporate ladder.

Fast forward three years when I gave birth to my second daughter, Gianna. As they say, this is where the rubber meets the road ladies and gentlemen. Holding down a high-profile job while taking care of a toddler and an infant became quite exhausting. My husband did as much as he could to help out, but he was traveling quite a bit. So things were chaotic, stressful and challenging to say the least.

With each passing month, I became less and less passionate about my career in corporate America. I knew my heart wasn't in it. I just didn't have that fire in my belly anymore. As a result, I knew I needed to take some time to do some real soul searching. It was time to bring this chapter to a close and start a new one in my life. One that I could be excited about. One that would make a greater impact on the world.

As luck would have it, my company was going through a restructuring. I thought to myself, *This is it! This is my chance to leave the corporate world and do something different!* I went down to my HR department and asked if they would consider including me in the restructuring. That afternoon, I walked out with a box of framed family photos and a six-month severance package.

I took some much needed time off to regroup and ultimately decided to start my private practice as a counselor/success coach. I was able to do this fairly easily because about nine years prior to being laid off, my company was very generous and agreed to pay for my Master's Degree in Counseling. That same year, I graduated from a four-year program at the Institute of Core Energetics where I specialized in energy psychology. Prior to having kids, this worked out really well. I was able to double dip, working my full-time job during the day and seeing clients at night.

So, becoming a counselor made a lot of sense to me. However, I underestimated how tough it would be. As any entrepreneur would tell you, building a business from scratch is no easy task! In fact, I've long since described my experience as jumping off the corporate ladder and landing in quicksand with a straitjacket on.

The entrepreneurial world is vastly different from the corporate world, and I wasn't prepared for the challenges I'd face. I thought that being an entrepreneur would allow me to spend a lot more quality time with my kids and accomplish that 'work-life balance' that I so desperately craved.

I couldn't have been more wrong.

I went from working fifty hours a week to eighty or more. I was attempting to build a business online. I spent hours and thousands of dollars trying to figure out how to do it, all at the expense of my family life.

I was hard-pressed to find any quality time with them. When I did, my mind was always spinning with all the things I needed to do, didn't do, and had to do to for my business - which at this point was really a very expensive, full-time hobby.

I'm thankful that I persevered and followed my dream. However, if I knew then what I know now, I would have done it differently. Very differently.

Now, I work with entrepreneurs, helping them avoid the mistakes I made so they can experience success in a cost-effective and productive way. I teach them how to truly live their dream of owning a successful business while being an amazing mom, wife, daughter, and friend.

Here's the advice I give my clients, and I hope that you will find it helpful as well.

1. Set and maintain well-defined boundaries. If you're working from home, then you run a huge risk of having your business take over your life. It's critical to establishing set work hours and stick to them. In addition, if you have the space, dedicate one area as your office and don't use it for anything else. This way you can leave your office when your workday is done. Otherwise, you'll find it extremely tempting to sit down and check your email for 'just a minute'. Then an hour and a half later, you realize you've missed the opportunity to tuck your kids into bed and kiss them good night.

2. Build a team. Working as a solopreneur can be counter-productive because you wind up working in your business (social media posts, blogging, record keeping, etc.) instead of on your business (finding clients, speaking at events, getting interviewed, etc.). This was a biggie for me. As a type-A, multitasking businesswoman on a budget, it was easy to justify doing all of it myself. However, it came at a big cost. My business didn't grow near as quickly as it could have. Once I decided I couldn't do it all myself, and enlisted some help, I was able to be more effective as a business owner and a mother.

    Teamwork makes the dream work. So, if you want to build a successful business build a team that can get behind you, assume some of the workload and help you succeed.

3. Practice Mindfulness. Most mompreneurs are great at multitasking, but it comes at a cost. When you try to balance being a mom and a successful mompreneur at once, you'll quickly discover that you won't do either very well. Before I figured this out, I shortchanged my kids big time.

I'd check my email or listen to voicemail messages while I was playing with them. Or I'd miss an important appointment while I was trying to soothe my crying child. By practicing mindfulness, you can focus on one thing at a time, giving it your full attention and ensure that nothing slips through the cracks.

4. Set goals. This seems so obvious, but I'm always amazed how many entrepreneurs don't set goals and just fly by the seat of their pants. I was one of them. When I was in the corporate world, I relied heavily on my planner and daily to-do list. Then when I became an entrepreneur, that habit went out the window.

   As they say, plan the work and work the plan! If you don't know where you're going, you'll go in circles getting nowhere fast. Be clear about what it is you want to accomplish then develop a strategy on how you'll get there and stick with it.

5. Know when to say no. As women, it's so easy to bite off more than we can chew, being the 'go-to gal' that will come to everyone's rescue. This is a very fast, effective way to burn yourself out.

   Be willing to say no to being the PTO president, Girl Scout troop leader, soccer mom, women's networking leader, neighborhood watch organizer...the list goes on and on. Be willing to say no and refuse to be everything to everyone. An important part of running a business is being a good decision maker. Learning to say no is a critical component of making good decisions.

6. Practice self-care. Trying to balance entrepreneurship and motherhood can make self-care very challenging. I learned the hard way that neglecting your physical and mental health can

take a toll on you and everyone around you. By taking care of yourself, you are better equipped to juggle competing priorities, handle stress and be there for those who need you. By eating right, exercising and unplugging mentally from time to time, you'll find that you're more effective at everything you do.

7.   Be true to who you are. This is your business, and you should be able to build it on your own terms. It's easy to lose your genuineness when you're modeling others who have been on this path before you. Always remember that you can achieve your goals and make your dreams come true by setting your own rules, writing your own playbook and being authentic and true to who you really are. You're a leader, not a follower and this is your opportunity to do it your way.

Starting your own business is very similar to having a baby. You begin with a seed, an idea of what you want to do. You go into labor bringing it to fruition, then you focus on nurturing it so that it grows and flourishes.

Trying to be successful at both can be quite challenging. At times, you may struggle to find harmony between the two roles of being a business owner and a mother. One may be momentarily overshadowed by the demands of the other.

However, if you adhere to the tips I've provided you, it is possible to have balance in your life and ensure that all of your babies (business and kids) thrive while you maintain your own sanity as well.

Lessons Learned and Mindset Tips

Lessons Learned:

1. Always stay true to who you are.

2. Know where you're going and determine how you're going to get there.

3. Always live life aligned with your personal values.

Mindset Tips:

1. Live in the here and now, focusing on one thing at a time.

2. Turn failures and setbacks into life lessons and apply what you've learned.

3. Be grateful for all that you have, even the smallest things in life.

Aha Moments and Self Reflections

Note your Thoughts

Conclusion

Your journey with us has come to an end...for now. We hope that you have discovered that we all have it in us to be an empowered momboss! *The Real journey of the Empowered Momboss* is a timeless one. You can be twenty or fifty-five years of age. Each step of our lives has prepared us for the next level of our journey, to share our knowledge with loved ones for generations to come. It is a journey of tenacity and perseverance. It is a personal journey, a not one size fits all description. It is about finding out what's working, and not working, for you and your family. It is about being real with yourself and your loved ones about what you need to succeed in your business and for your family to thrive. It involves asking yourself some very pointed questions, reworking schedules, and digging into your heart and soul to ignite the fire that gets you out of bed in the morning.

Open yourself up to the knowledge that there is a different path. It's about choice and understanding that although there may be obstacles in your path, there will also be unlimited opportunities. Self-discovery is a way of life, not a destination.

Our wish, as authors, is to inspire you to dig deep; find your passion and purpose, they are waiting to be unleashed to the world. The path may not be easy, but I have learned that one of the best questions to ask is, "What am I to learn from this experience?"

The stories shared with you are raw and vulnerable, from the heart and soul of each author. Each momboss overcame their obstacles so they could take their lives and businesses to a new level. With each chapter, we hope you learned new lessons and mindset tips that will allow you to reflect on your life through journaling in the notes pages.

There are many aspects to being a momboss. A strong sense of self-worth and knowing what fuels you is the foundation for a successful life and business. You must feel worthy and ready to receive all the blessings you deserve. It took me several thousands of dollars to figure out what I already knew deep within myself.

The world is shifting; women want the flexibility of working from home. This means more freedom, fun, and family stability. This is a paradigm shift and a movement to a new space.

We are all connected with communities wanting collaboration and a calling to pay it forward.

Life is a team sport, and so is being a momboss in the digital age.

Join us!
https://www.facebook.com/groups/empoweredmoms123/

"Together we can discover the quiet voice in you that knows this can be the last time. This time you succeed!"

–Heather Andrews

FOLLOW
IT THRU

After all the 'aha' moments and self-reflective journaling, my question for you is, are you ready to take action? You have read it here. Action makes passion. It creates momentum.

A few questions you may want to ask yourself are:

Are you a busy momboss who is trying to balance it all?

Do you feel stuck in the chaotic spin called life?

Are you a mom who wants it all?

Are you maxed out? Do you see no end to the daily grind of work, kids, and activities?

How did this happen? How did you get so tired that you could fall asleep at a stop light?

You are not alone!

I encourage you to stop for a moment and reflect on your feelings that occurred as you read the stories in this book and reflected on your own lessons learned and mindset tips. If you find yourself saying, "This is too hard" or "I can't do it by myself," then my answer is that you are not meant to do it on your own.

As a lifestyle strategist, and publisher and having lived my own momboss journey, I can tell you that there is a different way! There is a way for you to get a grip on the chaos, harness your energy, and build your business without sacrificing yourself or your family. You can have all the love, laugh, serenity and business success with a thriving family. You can do it by asking for support from your loved ones or friends. It might even involve hiring a mentor or enrolling in a course. The choice is yours.

I have been where you are, and I understand. There is a different path for you.

Let's talk!

Heather Andrews

www.followitthru.com
www.heatherandrews.press

Find other books by Follow it Thru Publishing on Amazon:

Obstacles Equal Opportunities

What's Self-Love Got to do With It? (Launches June 2018)